REJOICE IN ME

Other Books by David E. Rosage

Abide in Me
The Bread of Life
Climbing Higher
Follow Me
A Lenten Pilgrimage
Listen to Him
The Lord is My Shepherd
Speak, Lord, Your Servant Is Listening

Rejoice in Me

A Pocket Guide to Daily Scriptural Prayer

David E. Rosage

SERVANT BOOKS
Ann Arbor, Michigan

Front cover photograph by Ed Cooper
Back cover author portrait by Howard M. DeCruyenaere

Published by Servant Books
P.O. Box 8617
Ann Arbor, Michigan 48107

87 88 89 90 91 92 10 9 8 7 6 5 4 3 2 1

Printed in the United States of America

ISBN 0-89283-364-5

Library of Congress Cataloging-in-Publication Data

Rosage, David E.
  Rejoice in me.

  1. Devotional calendars—Catholic Church.
2. Bible. O.T. Psalms—Meditations.   I. Title.
BX2182.2.R66 1986   242'.2   86-15592
ISBN 0-89283-364-5

Contents

Dedicated to
King David and all the other authors of
the psalms
who were docile to the Spirit
and bequeathed us
the psalter as a most precious heritage

Introduction

THIS PSALM DEVOTIONAL IS THE THIRD and final book in a series of prayer programs or guides offering a scriptural prayer outline for each day of the year. This volume differs from the other two books, *Follow Me* and *Abide in Me,* in that the basis of every day's prayer is taken from the psalms. The psalms have a power within them to waken in our hearts a desire and a longing for a more personal and a more prayerful relationship with our loving Father.

At times all of us feel an urgency and a duty to praise, thank, and glorify God for his majesty and magnificence. At the same time we experience our own inadequacy to express the real sentiments of admiration and adoration or reverence and gratitude which fill our hearts.

The Hebrews of old had a similar experience, but under the inspiration and guidance of the Holy Spirit certain persons were able to give expression to these interior sentiments by composing songs of praise which we call psalms. Their cries of wonder and exultation, of anguish and joy, of praise and thanksgiving expressed in these psalms inspire and motivate us into joyously singing of the praises of our gracious God.

God's Songs

The Book of Psalms is a collection of songs of a people who knew God with their hearts. They experienced God's faithfulness in his might and mercy, in his loving care and concern, in his power and protection. When they felt threatened or in dire need, they cried out in supplication, confident that God in his kindness would come to their rescue, which he invariably did.

The chosen people tried to verbalize their contemplative experience of God by praising, thanking, and glorifying him. These songs of joy and gratitude became what we call the Psalter. The heritage which they left us is the only book of divinely inspired prayers we have.

The psalms do not lead us into a speculative theology about God. The Psalter is rather a compendium of God's revelation of himself and his attributes. The Psalter is a garden enclosing fruits from all the other books of the Bible. If all the books of the Old Testament were lost, we would still have a substantial framework of God's revelation of himself and of salvation history in the psalms alone, the Psalter contains the human and divine history of the chosen people expressed in religious songs. It is a summary of both the Old Testament and the New Testament. Of the approximately three hundred quotes of the Old Testament found in the New Testament, one-third of them are from the psalms.

Jesus loved the psalms. In the home at Nazareth, Jesus prayed the psalms with Mary and Joseph every morning and evening, at every meal, and on feast days. In his public life he prayed the psalms when he went to the synagogue as he was in the custom of doing. He prayed them with the apostles at the last supper and again on the cross. Today the church uses the psalms extensively in her eucharistic liturgy, in the liturgy of the hours, in the administration of the sacraments, and in many other prayers.

Our Prayer

As we pray the psalms we, too, will discover God as the Lord and Master of the universe who guides the destiny of nations, controls the seas, the sun, moon, and stars, calling each one by name. Even more we will become more deeply aware of his abiding presence and fidelity, of his loving care and concern for each one of us as our loving Father. St. Athanasius says: "The psalms are the best way to praise God and the fitting words in which to bless him."

The psalms will help us to rejoice with the Lord, to praise him, to thank him, and to petition him for our needs. In the psalms we will find hope and reassurance. They will be the source of much comfort and consolation in distress.

The psalms have the power to lift us up out of our workaday world with all its competitive demands and bring us into the loving presence of our Father.

Format

This psalm devotional offers a prayer reflection for each day of the year, arranged in fifty-two weeks. Each week has its own special theme. Every fourth week in this series has a recurring theme of praise of God.

One or several verses of a psalm set the central thought for each day, which is followed by a brief commentary designed to stimulate some reflection on the theme. The daily prayer concludes with a scriptural passage, usually from the New Testament, which may expand or confirm the theme of that day.

How to Use This Book

This psalm devotional is a kind of launching pad enabling a person to enter into meditative or contemplative prayer. It is intended for those who desire to enrich their own relationship with the Lord and especially for those who feel they have little time for formal prayer. The following procedure is suggested:

1. Read the psalm verse slowly and prayerfully. Let every word find a home in your heart.

2. Pause and rest with a word or phrase which may resonate within you.

3. After you have absorbed the central thought of the psalm verse, then read the commentary reflectively.

4. After some time spent in reflection, read the scriptural passage which follows. It will corroborate and expand the theme of the day.

5. You may wish to underline a word or expression to which you can easily revert throughout the day. Even better, keep a little journal in which you jot down a word or expression which you wish to ponder from time to time.

6. It may be profitable for a better understanding of a psalm to read the whole psalm in the Bible. It may happen that an excerpt taken out of context may not be readily appreciated.

> Praise the Lord, for he is good;
>> sing praise to our God, for he is gracious;
>> it is fitting to praise him.

Psalm 147:1

As We Begin

PSALM 131 INTRODUCES US to an ideal posture for entering into prayer. An inordinate longing for honors, status, power, or wealth will make it impossible for us to establish a personal and intimate relationship with the Lord in prayer.

A "weaned child" resting on its mother's lap speaks volumes about the ideal attitude for prayer. It expresses a childlike trust and gratitude to God for the security and satisfaction which we find in our loving Father.

Jesus himself explained the ideal attitude and disposition:

> "I assure you, unless you change and become like little children, you will not enter the kingdom of God. Whoever makes himself lowly, becoming like this child, is of greatest importance in that heavenly reign." (Mt 18:3-4)

As we pray with the psalmist, we will more readily enter into a proper disposition for prayer. When the divinely inspired sentiments and words of this psalm find a home in our hearts, then we are moving into a rich, prayerful relationship with the Lord, in which we may experience his loving presence.

17

Humble Trust in God

O Lord, my heart is not proud,
   nor are my eyes haughty;
   I busy not myself with great things,
   nor with things too sublime for me.

Nay rather, I have stilled and quieted
   my soul like a weaned child.
   Like a weaned child on its mother's lap
   so is my soul within me.

O Israel, hope in the Lord,
   both now and forever.
                Psalm 131

Part I

Lord, Teach Us to Pray.

(Lk 11:1)

Prayer of Listening

The Lord is calling us into the prayer of listening. The psalmist certainly encourages us to pray in this fashion. How frequently the inspired writer bids us to be quiet, to listen, to wait for the Lord in silence.

We cannot love a person we do not know, and we cannot know a person to whom we have not listened. Listening prayer means meeting the Lord at the depth of our being. Listening is "wasting time with the Lord." Listening is loving. Listening is praying.

1 Psalm 37:7 Waiting Is Praying
Leave it to the Lord, / and wait for him.

In the prayer of listening, we pause, relax, and rest in the Lord's presence. We try to be attentive to him. We strive to listen to discover his will. We give ourselves totally to him.

Complete abandonment to the Lord's will— waiting to do, or be, whatever he wishes—is an attitude conducive to the prayer of the heart.

Mary, our Mother, is our model of total abandonment: "I am the servant of the Lord. Let it be done to me as you say." (Lk 1:38)

2 Psalm 46:11-12   Awareness Pause
Desist! and confess that I am God, / exalted among the nations, exalted upon the earth. / The Lord of hosts is with us; / our stronghold is the God of Jacob.

Desist reminds us of the age-old warning at a railroad crossing:

STOP   LOOK   LISTEN

The Lord says, "Stop your busyness. Look around you at my beauty reflected in creation. Listen as I am telling you how much I love you."

The Father bids us to pause and listen: "Come to me heedfully, listen, that you may have life." (Is 55:3)

3 Psalm 62:2-3   Prayer of the Heart
Only in God is my soul at rest; / from him comes my salvation. / He only is my rock and my salvation, / my stronghold; I shall not be disturbed at all.

In our prayer of listening we discover the tranquil assurance that God, in his boundless love for us, will protect us and lead us safely to our salvation.

Since only God is our rock and our stronghold, our trust should be so great that nothing could disturb us, and our soul will be at rest.

Jesus leads us into this kind of prayer by his own example: "When he had sent them away, he went up on the mountain by himself to pray." (Mt 14:23)

4 Psalm 95:7b-8a   Open Heart
O, that today you would hear his voice: / "Harden not your hearts."

The psalmist makes this urgent appeal that we not only listen to the voice of the Lord but that we take it to heart and put it into practice.

St. James's advice also contains a note of urgency: "Humbly welcome the word that has taken root in you, with its power to save you. Act on this word. If all you do is listen to it, you are deceiving yourselves." (Jas 1:21-22)

The Father's admonition to us is brief, but direct: "Listen to him." (Mt 17:5)

5 Psalm 119:99   Heart Knowledge
I have more understanding than all my teachers / when your decrees are my meditation.

Prayer of the heart leads us into deeper insights and a richer understanding and knowledge of God than we could ever achieve intellectually.

This kind of prayer requires regular, prolonged quiet in the sunshine of the Lord's loving presence.

This was the prayer of Mary our Mother: "Mary treasured all these things and reflected on them in her heart." (Lk 2:19)

6 Psalm 38:14 and 16   Sounds of Silence

I am like a deaf man, hearing not, / like a dumb man who opens not his mouth. / Because for you, O Lord, I wait; / you, O Lord my God, will answer.

In order to be solely attentive to the Lord, the prayer of listening requires that we try to turn off our gift of hearing "like a deaf man, hearing not" and likewise refrain from speaking "like a dumb man who opens not his mouth." We need to rest quietly in his presence as if we were taking a sunbath in the radiance of his presence.

This prayer of the heart demands only that we be receptive to the influence of the Lord's divine presence and love. Jesus instructs us in these words: "Whenever you pray, go to your room, close your door, and pray to your Father in private." (Mt 6:6)

7 Psalm 141:2   Ascending Fragrance

Let my prayer come like incense before you; / the lifting up of my hands, like the evening sacrifice.

As we observe the fragrant smoke of incense rising noiselessly and effortlessly heavenward, we can visualize our prayer, like the incense, wafting its way toward the throne of God. A draft or a breeze could easily disturb the sweet-smelling smoke from ascending quietly upward. Likewise, inordinate attachments, pride, or willful distractions could be compared to such a draft preventing our prayers from going heavenward without interference. The sacred writer urges us to: "Send up the sweet odor of incense, / break forth in blossoms like the lily. / Send up the sweet odor of your hymn of praise; / bless the Lord for all he has done!" (Sir 39:14)

Waiting on the Lord

Waiting in scriptural usage does not simply mean marking time but rather a waiting on the Lord.

In some instances it may mean conditioning and preparing ourselves for the coming of the Lord.

At other times it may mean waiting on the Lord like a waiter or waitress waits upon guests in a public dining room or restaurant.

Waiting is being for the Lord.

Waiting is praying.

1 Psalm 25:5   Waiting Rewards

Guide me in your truth and teach me, / for you are God my savior, / and for you I wait all the day.

The Lord teaches and guides us in his truth by molding, fashioning, and transforming our heart. There he gives us insights far beyond our human comprehension.

There is one important condition. We must listen. When we spend time in the prayer of listening, we are waiting—waiting for the Lord.

Jesus invites us to join him and the apostles: "Come by yourselves to an out-of-the-way place and rest a little." (Mk 6:31)

2 Psalm 25:21   Waiting Transforms
Let integrity and uprightness preserve me, / because I wait for you, O Lord.

Adhering honestly and conscientiously to a set of moral values will give us the "integrity and uprightness" of a true follower of Jesus.

This kind of waiting empowers us to be effective disciples reflecting his love, peace, and joy to all who cross our path.

Jesus' sage advice is important: "Remain here in the city until you are clothed with power from on high." (Lk 24:49)

3 Psalm 27:14   Waiting Builds Courage
Wait for the Lord with courage; / be stouthearted, and wait for the Lord.

When the woman with the hemorrhage waited only to touch the tassel of his cloak, Jesus took the occasion to say: "Courage, daughter! Your faith has restored you to health". (Mt 9:20ff)

As we wait for the Lord, we, too, will find courage and be stouthearted when problems and pains, difficulties or defeats confront us.

Even if we abandon him, Jesus tells us not to fear: "I tell you all this / that in me you may find peace. / You will suffer in the world. / But take courage! / I have overcome the world." (Jn 16:33)

4 Psalm 37:34   Wait in Patience
Wait for the Lord, / and keep his way.

Waiting for the Lord does not mean simply listening for his words. It also means being receptive and pliable in his hands for whatever task he may be preparing us.

Isaiah used an apt figure of speech: "We are the clay and you the potter: we are all the work of your hands" (Is 64:7).

Jesus tells us to wait for the Holy Spirit: "Wait, rather, for the fulfillment of my Father's promise, of which you have heard me speak." (Acts 1:4)

5 Psalm 39:8-9   Waiting Expresses Hope
And now, for what do I wait, O Lord? / In you is my hope. / From all my sins deliver me; / a fool's taunt let me not suffer.

Waiting for the Lord brings us to a genuine heart-knowledge of our loving Father in whom we can place all our trust.

When we quietly and prayerfully wait for the Lord, we discover him as the source of all our hope.

St. Paul prays for us: "So may God, the source of hope, fill you with all joy and peace in believing so that through the power of the Holy Spirit you may have hope in abundance." (Rom 15:13)

6 Psalm 40:2-3 Trustful Waiting
I have waited, waited for the Lord, / and he stooped toward me and heard my cry. / He drew me out of the pit of destruction, / out of the mud of the swamp; / He set my feet upon a crag; / he made firm my steps.

Jesus came into our world to lift us out of the miry swamp of our sinfulness. He came to reveal his Father's and his own loving mercy and compassion.

We need to wait upon him by humbly acknowledging our brokenness and our need for his healing and forgiveness.

Jesus explains why he came: "I have not come to invite the self-righteous to a change of heart, but sinners." (Lk 5:32)

7 Psalm 130:6 Watchful Waiting
My soul waits for the Lord / more than sentinels wait for the dawn.

How eagerly the guard on night duty waits for the dawn. Daylight makes it easier to detect and ward off any danger lurking nearby. We always feel safer in the light of day.

Reminding ourselves that we are always in the presence of the Lord gives us the reassurance of his powerful protection and his providential love for each one of us.

We borrow this thought from one of St. Paul's discourses: "In him we live and move and have our being . . . for we too are his offspring." (Acts 17:28)

Meeting the Lord at Dawn

Spiritual writers have always encouraged the early morning hour as an ideal time for prayer. Dawn is the beginning of a new day—a new phase on our journey through life to our heavenly home. We do not journey alone. The Lord is always with us. How appropriate that we spend some time with him each morning, planning and preparing for the day's journey.

1 Psalm 5:3b-4   Prime Time

To you I pray, O Lord; / at dawn you hear my voice; / at dawn I bring my plea expectantly before you.

Dawn is that intervening period between the darkness of night and the fullness of the daylight.

This symbolizes our spiritual growth. We have left the darkness of sin, but we have not yet reached the eternal glory. Dawn is an ongoing process leading us to the brilliance of eternal life.

Morning prayer gives us inspiration and motivation. It gives a lilt and joy to our whole day.

Jesus showed us the way: "Rising early next morning, he went off to a lonely place in the desert; there he was absorbed in prayer." (Mk 1:35)

2 Psalm 57:9-10
Morning Praise   Morning Thanks

Awake, O my soul; awake, lyre and harp! / I will wake the dawn. / I will give thanks to you among the peoples, O Lord. / I will chant your praise among the nations.

Someone said: "Providence arises even before the sun." One of the myriad blessings of God's providential love is the gift of oxygen which kept us alive during our hours of slumber.

Realizing that we respire over one thousand times each hour, should not our morning prayer be one of thanksgiving for the gift of life?

St. Paul expresses the sentiments of the psalmist in these words: "Rejoice always, never cease praying, render constant thanks; such is God's will for you in Christ Jesus." (1 Thes 5:16-17)

3 Psalm 88:14   Morning Waiting

But I, O Lord, cry out to you; / with my morning prayer I wait upon you.

The morning hours are usually filled with frantic activity as we begin a new day.

Arising a little before the deadline to "wait upon the Lord" to discover what he asks of us this day will bring much peace and calm to what might otherwise be a hectic beginning.

Waiting upon the Lord may be even more refreshing than that first cup of coffee.

Jesus wants us to come to him with our morning prayer: "Come to me, all you who are weary and find life burdensome, and I will refresh you." (Mt 11:28)

4 Psalm 90:14-15
Beginning the Day with Joy

Fill us at daybreak with your kindness, / that we may shout for joy and gladness all our days. / Make us glad, for the days when you afflicted us, / for the years when we saw evil.

Each new day we need to remind ourselves that we are living in the "eternal now" of God where he is eternally the same—loving us, inspiring us, sustaining us, energizing us.

Afflictions bring us to an awareness of our needs and of his abiding presence with us to meet those needs.

St. Peter's reminder also helps us: "In the Lord's eyes, one day is as a thousand years and a thousand years are as a day." (2 Pt 3:8)

5 Psalm 92:2-3 Morning Proclamation

It is good to give thanks to the Lord, / to sing praise to your name, Most High, / To proclaim your kindness at dawn / and your faithfulness throughout the night.

At the beginning of each new day we are reminded of God's boundless goodness to us. He not only gives us life but also supplies all the needs we have to survive.

Even more, he shares his divine life with us as a foretaste of our total union with him in heaven.

No wonder Paul advises us: "Whatever you do, whether in speech or in action, do it in the name of the Lord Jesus. Give thanks to God the Father through him." (Col 3:17)

6 Psalm 119:146-147 Plea at Dawn

I call upon you; save me, / and I will keep your decrees. / Before dawn I come and cry out; / I hope in your words.

The duties and demands which challenge us at the beginning of each new day would certainly unnerve us. They keep us aware of our own inability and our own inadequacy to cope with all the happenings of the day.

Realizing the loving presence and power of the Lord with us enkindles our hope and enboldens us to face each task.

We find great encouragement in the word of the Lord: "Rejoice in hope, be patient under trial, persevere in prayer." (Rom 12:12)

7 Psalm 143:8
Beginning the Day with the Lord

At dawn let me hear of your kindness, / for in you I trust. / Show me the way in which I should walk, / for to you I lift up my soul.

Jesus rose from the dead early in the morning to reveal a way of life in which we should walk. He assured us that he would never leave us but would always remain with us in his resurrected, glorified life.

Each morning as we renew our faith in his presence, we will discover great consolation.

St. Paul says it so well: "The life I live now is not my own; Christ is living in me." (Gal 2:20)

Let Us Praise the Lord

I n the format of this booklet, you will discover that the theme of each fourth week will encourage us to sing the praises of the Lord.

Praise is a high form of prayer since it is God-centered. Praise lifts our minds and hearts above the mundane concerns of this life and upward to our loving Father, the Lord and Master of the entire universe. In our prayer we become absorbed solely in praising and glorifying our Father, the God of heaven and earth.

1 Psalm 16:7 and 9   Direct Line

I bless the Lord who counsels me; / even in the night my heart exhorts me. / Therefore my heart is glad and my soul rejoices, / my body, too, abides in confidence.

The Lord counsels us by giving us insights and inspiration, by transforming our hearts and minds, by influencing our actions and attitudes.

Think of the sublime privilege which is ours. The transcendent God of heaven and earth wants to communicate with us. When we consider how difficult it is for us to get even a brief visit with an important person, then we can appreciate having the Lord at our beck and call. We want to say: "Praise and glory, wisdom and thanksgiving and honor, power and might, to our God forever and ever. Amen!" (Rev 7:12)

2 Psalm 29:3-4 The Lord Is Majestic
The voice of the Lord is over the waters, / the God of glory thunders, / the Lord, over vast waters. / The voice of the Lord is mighty; / the voice of the Lord is majestic.

Imagine yourself standing on a beach and listening to the thunderous dashing of the waves against the rocks, which reveals the might of God's power. The expansiveness of the "vast waters" reminds us of the immensity of God. The rhythm of the waves creates a spectacular scene of God's majesty. When Jesus showed his almighty power in calming the sea, Mark tells us: "A great awe overcame them at this. They kept saying to one another, 'Who can this be that the wind and the sea obey him?'" (Mk 4:41)

3 Psalm 63:5 Hands Uplifted
Thus will I bless you while I live; / lifting up my hands, I will call upon your name.

In this prayer we call upon the name of the Lord with hands uplifted. Lifting up our hands is a gesture, which intensifies our desire and makes our prayer more fervent. Body language helps us to enter more fervently into prayer. We have all experienced the Lord's gracious response in the past. This makes us even more confident that he will continue to respond when we call upon his name. This conviction impels us to bless the Lord while we live. St. Paul makes his wishes known to us: "It is my wish, then, that in every place the men shall offer prayers with blameless hands held aloft, and be free from anger and dissension." (1 Tim 2:8)

4 Psalm 111:10 Genuine Wisdom
The fear of the Lord is the beginning of wisdom; / prudent are all who live by it. / His praise endures forever.

We remind ourselves that the "fear of the Lord" means a reverence for God. Fear is the Hebrew form for our word, religion—our relationship with our heavenly Father. We live this relationship when we say a brief "Thank you, Lord," or admire the beauty of nature, or enjoy the love of a dear one. A very powerful means of expressing this relationship is to praise God always. Jesus teaches that the beginning of wisdom is love, especially the love of our enemies. He says: "This will prove that you are sons of your heavenly Father, for his sun rises on the bad and the good, he rains on the just and the unjust." (Mt 5:45)

5 Psalm 115:17-18 Bless the Lord
It is not the dead who praise the Lord, / nor those who go down into silence; / But we bless the Lord, / both now and forever.

The sacrament of the moment is the most important time of our whole life. What happened in the past or what the future holds in store for us is beyond our control. The disposition and attitude of our heart and mind at this moment is all important to the Lord. If our hearts are filled with the praises of the Lord, the present moment becomes precious to us and pleasing to the Lord. Tobit's advice is noteworthy: "At all times bless the Lord God, and ask him to make all your paths straight and to grant success to all your endeavors and plans." (Tb 4:19)

6 Psalm 123:1 and 2b
Enthroned in Heaven

To you I lift up my eyes / who are enthroned in heaven. / So are our eyes on the Lord, our God, / till he have pity on us.

When we fix our mind's eye on the Lord, we are moving into an attitude of quiet prayer. As we visualize the Lord "enthroned in heaven" we are filled with awe and wonder. It is then our hearts become jubilant, and we yearn to sing his praises.

When our eyes are on the Lord our God, we are praying. As our voices reecho his praise, as we glorify his name, our Father is pleased. St. Peter explains it thus: "Your adornment is rather the hidden character of the heart, expressed in the unfading beauty of a calm and gentle disposition. This is precious in God's eyes." (1 Pt 3:4)

7 Psalm 134:1 Quiet Time
Come, bless the Lord, / all you servants of the Lord, / who stand in the house of the Lord, / during the hours of night.

We are invited to come and bless the Lord "during the hours of the night" when the noise and confusion of the day simmers down. In the quiet hours of the night we find the solitude and stillness which is so conducive to prayer.

As we reflect on the countless blessings of the day just passed, our hearts want to ring out the praises of the Lord.

Jesus found the nocturnal hours conducive to prayer: "He went out to the mountain to pray, spending the night in communion with God." (Lk 6:12)

Part II

Everything God Created Is Good.

(1 Tm 4:4)

Love Fashions and Shares

Genesis relates the story of creation as an historical narrative, while Psalm 104 tells the story in beautiful poetic imagery. Creation is an expression of God's love. His creation is ongoing. It is a sharing of himself. The love of husband and wife expressed in procreation is a reflection of God's creative love. With the psalmist, let us praise the power and wisdom of our creating Father.

1 Psalm 104:1-2a   Creator of Light
Bless the Lord, O my soul! / O Lord, my God, you are great indeed! / You are clothed with majesty and glory, / robed in light as with a cloak.

On the first day of creation God said: "'Let there be light,' and there was light" (Gn 1:3). Light has always been the symbol of the presence and glory of God. "God made the two great lights, the greater one to govern the day, and the lesser one to govern the night; and he made the stars" (Gn 1:16). The immensity of the sun, moon, and stars baffles our imagination, but compared to the God of Light they are infinitesimal. Jesus explains the power of divine light: "I am the light of the world. / No follower of mine shall ever walk in darkness; / no, he shall possess the light of life." (Jn 8:12)

2 Psalm 104:5-6a   Marvels of His Creation

You fixed the earth upon its foundation, / not to be moved forever; / With the ocean, as with a garment, you covered it.

If we stand on a beach and try to imagine the immensity of the ocean, we begin to comprehend the marvels of God's creative power. We recall that our planet is only a small part of the entire universe. Why did God create such marvels? God created to manifest his love and for the enjoyment of his creatures. St. Paul's comment is right to the point: "For us there is one God, the Father, from whom all things come and for whom we live; and one Lord Jesus Christ through whom everything was made and through whom we live." (1 Cor 8:6)

3 Psalm 104:13-14a
God's Creative Love Provides

You water the mountains from your palace; / the earth is replete with the fruit of your works. / You raise the grass for the cattle, / and vegetation for men's use.

Another dimension of God's love is his boundless providence. He cares so much that he meets every need for our welfare. A brief sojourn in a barren desert would bring us to a deeper appreciation of God's care and concern. Jesus told us of the Father's loving concern: "Your Father knows that you need such things. Seek out instead his kingship over you, and the rest will follow in turn." (Lk 12:30-31)

4 Psalm 104:19-20a   Sun and Moon

You made the moon to mark the seasons; / the sun knows the hour of its setting. / You bring darkness, and it is night.

The brilliance of the sun illumines the day, enabling us to work and recreate in its pleasant light. The reflective light of the moon providentially mitigates the darkness of night for our convenience and enjoyment. Knowing our human needs, God arranged the rhythm of day and night for man's work and rest. "The city had no need of sun or moon, for the glory of God gave it light, and its lamp was the Lamb." (Rev 21:23)

5 Psalm 104:24-25
The Sea Is His Handiwork

How manifold are your works, O Lord! / In wisdom you have wrought them all— / the earth is full of your creatures; / The sea also, great and wide, / in which are schools without number / of living things both small and great.

The grandeur and immensity of the sea reflects the mystery of God. The thunderous roaring, the towering waves, the fathomless depths, the endless expanse, and the vast variety of marine life manifest the power and beauty of God's creative love. May we stand in awe and reverence before his handiwork realizing that earth, with all its magnificence, is but a dim shadow of his majesty. Jesus' disciples recognized his divine power over the water: "What sort of man is this," they said, "that even the winds and sea obey him?" (Mt 8:27)

6 Psalm 104:30 Man, God's Masterpiece

When you send forth your spirit, they are created, / and you renew the face of the earth.

"'Let us make man in our image, after our likeness.'.... God created man in his image; in the divine image he created him" (Gn 1:26-27). Man is the masterpiece of God's creative love. God endowed man with intelligence and understanding and shared his own divine life with us by filling us with his Spirit. He loves us so much that he shared himself with us by the power of his Spirit. St. Paul reminds us of our re-creation: "... if anyone is in Christ, he is a new creation. The old order has passed away; now all is new!" (2 Cor 5:17)

7 Psalm 104:31-33 Sing the Glory of God's Creation

May the glory of the Lord endure forever; / may the Lord be glad in his works! / He who looks upon the earth, and it trembles; / who touches the mountains, and they smoke! / I will sing to the Lord all my life; / I will sing praise to my God while I live.

All of the creation we behold is only one tiny facet of God's infinite creative love. This awareness fills our hearts with such joy that we, too, say: "I will sing to the Lord all my life; I will sing praise to my God while I live." Let us pray with St. John: "O Lord our God, you are worthy /to receive glory and honor and power! / For you have created all things; / by your will they came to be and were made." (Rev 4:11)

Love Creates and Recreates

Throughout Scripture we find the statement "God made the heavens and the earth." This is just another way of saying God's love is creative. Since heaven and earth is the handiwork of God, we should have great reverence and respect for every phase of his creation. Our contemplation of creation will instill in us a greater appreciation of God's creative love as well as awe and reverence for his magnificent works.

1 Psalm 139:13-14 Wonderfully Made
Truly you have formed my inmost being; / you knit me in my mother's womb. / I give you thanks that I am fearfully, wonderfully made; / wonderful are your works.

Love by nature wants to give. By the mutual love of husband and wife, God creates within a mother a new life which will live for all eternity. Even a momentary reflection will help us realize how wonderfully we are made and endowed with so many gifts, such as seeing, hearing, understanding, and speaking. Surely his works are wonderful. "We are truly his handiwork, created in Christ Jesus to lead the life of good deeds which God prepared for us in advance." (Eph 2:10)

2 Psalm 89:48   Fragile Sojourn
Remember how short my life is; / how frail you created all the children of men!

The psalmist reminds us how short is our earthly sojourn and how fragile is our natural life. Our next heartbeat, like the last one, is a gift from God. Our benevolent Father gives each one of us sufficient time to come to know him in this land of exile, to discover his way of life and our special mission here on earth. All this is a preparation for a life of perfect bliss which is eternal. St. Paul's counsel is right to the point: "May I never boast of anything but the cross of our Lord Jesus Christ! .. . All that matters is that one is created anew. Peace and mercy on all who follow this rule of life." (Gal 6:14-16)

3 Psalm 8:4-5   Magnificent Masterpiece
When I behold your heavens, the work of your fingers, / the moon and the stars which you set in place— / What is man that you should be mindful of him, / or the son of man that you should care for him?

We are the masterpiece of God's creative love. Our mission is to reflect his glory and give him the honor and praise which his handiwork deserves. The people we meet, are also very special masterpieces of God's creative love. It behooves us to recognize and respect them as such. Rejoice with the inspired writer: "Yours, O Lord, are grandeur and power, / majesty, splendor, and glory." (1 Chr 29:11)

4 Psalm 115:15-16   Only a Shadow
May you be blessed by the Lord, / who made heaven and earth. / Heaven is the heaven of the Lord, / but the earth he has given to the children of men.

This is a fervent prayer for a tremendous blessing—the blessing of the Lord of heaven and earth. God created the earth just for us. Let us stand and gaze in wonder at the beauty and the bounty of God's creation surrounding and enveloping us. Yet this is only a shadow of "what God has prepared for those who love him" (1 Cor 2:9). Listen to Jesus' invitation: "Come. You have my Father's blessing! Inherit the kingdom prepared for you from the creation of the world." (Mt 25:34)

5 Psalm 119:73   Ongoing Creation
Your hands have made me and fashioned me; / give me discernment that I may learn your commands.

In this prayer we ask God, whose love fashioned us, to endow us with the gift of discernment that we may learn his commands and know his will. God's commands are not merely rules and regulations to curtail our freedom; rather they are directives, given in love, to guide us on our journey back to our Father. St. Paul explains the fruit of discernment in these words: "What you have done is put aside your old self with its past deeds and put on a new man, one who grows in knowledge as he is formed anew in the image of his Creator." (Col 3:9-10)

6 Psalm 121:1-2   Faithful Creator

I lift up my eyes toward the mountains; / whence shall help come to me? / My help is from the Lord, / who made heaven and earth.

The ancient Hebrews regarded the top of the mountains as the special abiding place of God. To keep their vision fixed on eternal values, they raised their eyes to the mountain top. If we lift our eyes "toward the mountains" we are going directly to the very source of our help, the Lord, the Creator of heaven and earth. St. Peter's advice is sound: "Let those who suffer as God's will requires continue in good deeds, and entrust their lives to a faithful Creator." (1 Pt 4:19)

7 Psalm 146:5-6   Created in God's Image

Happy he whose help is the God of Jacob, / whose hope is in the Lord, his God, / Who made heaven and earth, / the sea and all that is in them.

When we contemplate the mighty power of the Lord our God, who created the heavens and earth as well as the sea with its myriad forms of life, we have reason for a firm hope. Hope is the source of our happiness, peace, and joy. A little spark of hope is enkindled and fanned into a mighty conflagration as we strive to put on the image of Jesus by living the Gospel message. St. Paul's advice is certainly direct: "Acquire a fresh, spiritual way of thinking. You must put on that new man created in God's image, whose justice and holiness are born of truth." (Eph 4:23-24)

The Work of Your Fingers

God's creative love surrounds us. We behold its beauty and bounty. We touch its solidity and softness. We smell its fragrance and freshness. We savor its taste and sweetness.

His creative love is dynamic and operative within us energizing us and enabling us to function. His creative love is ongoing, healing us and keeping us healthy. One caution sign we all need to observe. We can easily take his love for granted. We have need to keep ourselves aware of his enduring and faithful love.

1 Psalm 96:4-5   No Other
For great is the Lord and highly to be praised; / awesome is he, beyond all gods. / For all the gods of the nations are things of nought, / but the Lord made the heavens.

In our technological age we can easily begin to pay homage to the false gods of our quasi-miraculous accomplishments devised by the minds of men and women. Our computerized society is proud of its achievements—so colossal that some people begin to doubt the necessity of a supreme being.

On the other hand, a simple reflection of the vastness and beauty of creation will quickly bring us back to the reality and the necessity of a Creator who fashioned heaven and earth.

The angel in John's vision advises us: "Honor God and give him glory, for his time has come to sit in judgment. Worship the Creator of heaven and earth, the Creator of the sea and the springs." (Rev 14:7)

47

2 Psalm 33:6-7   Might and Majesty
By the word of the Lord the heavens were made; / by the breath of his mouth all their host. / He gathers the waters of the sea as in a flask; / in cellars he confines the deep.

In this hymn of praise we recall the might and majesty of the Creator of the universe. He created the highest heaven with their host of countless stars. His power reaches the very depth of the ocean.

Imagine yourself at the beach on a clear night with the stars blinking their hymn of praise and the ocean adding its thunderous voice of praise. Let your soul rise heavenward to glorify God's power.

Reflect with St. John: "Through him all things came into being, / and apart from him nothing came to be. / Whatever came to be in him, found life, / life for the light of men." (Jn 1:3-4)

3 Psalm 33:8-9   Re-creation
Let all the earth fear the Lord; / let all who dwell in the world revere him. / For he spoke, and it was made; / he commanded, and it stood forth.

The entire universe and all the mystery which it holds was created by an act of the will of God. "He spoke, and it was made."

We, too, were in the mind of God from all eternity. His love called us into being at this designated time. By his redemption, Jesus re-created us. His abiding presence with us continues the process of re-creation within us.

St. Paul's summary is full of meaning: "In him everything in heaven and on earth was created, things visible and invisible, whether thrones or dominations, principalities or powers; all were created through him, and for him. . . . In him everything continues in being." (Col 1:16-17)

4 **Psalm 89:12-13a   Omnipresent Love**
Yours are the heavens, and yours is the earth; / the world and its fullness you have founded; / North and south you created.

When we behold the multiplicity of fruits and flowers, of animals large and small, of trees tall and ornamental, of glittering stars and the brilliant sun, we cannot refrain from praising and glorifying the Lord of all creation.

The massive mountains and the luscious valleys with streams of fresh water meandering through them all bespeaks the grandeur and the glory of God. Yet all the beauty of nature is but a faint reflection of the beauty of God.

Pray with St. Paul: "To the King of ages, the immortal, the invisible, the only God, be honor and glory forever and ever! Amen." (1 Tm 1:17)

5 **Psalm 8:2   Meditative Moment**
O Lord, our Lord, / how glorious is your name over all the earth! / You have exalted your majesty above the heavens.

God's beauty, majesty, and glory are displayed in all his creation. Pause momentarily at times to observe and enjoy some work of his creative genius.

Behold a gorgeous sunset, a mountain silhouette at eventide, the dexterity of your hand, the gift of sight, and, indeed, the universe in all its parts.

St. Paul points out the divinity of Jesus: "He has put all things under Christ's feet and has made him, thus exalted, head of the church, which is his body: the fullness of him who fills the universe in all its parts." (Eph 1:22-23)

6 Psalm 95:6-7 King of Creation

Come, let us bow down in worship; / let us kneel before the Lord who made us. / For he is our God, / and we are the people he shepherds, the flock he guides.

In the Liturgy of the Hours, we are daily invited to praise and worship the Lord because he is the King of creation and we are his handiwork. Our recognition of him as Creator fills us with sentiments of wonder and gratitude.

He deserves our praise and worship because his creative love is ongoing, providing all our needs with the loving concern of a shepherd.

In the prologue to his Gospel John reminds us: "He was in the world, and through him the world was made, yet the world did not know who he was." (Jn 1:10)

7 Psalm 148:5-6 Mysterious Designs

Let them praise the name of the Lord, / for he commanded and they were created; / He established them forever and ever; / he gave them a duty which shall not pass away.

We can readily recognize the wisdom and the power of God, our Creator, in the order and design we find in the world. We discover his divine plan in the rhythm of the seasons, in the night which follows day, in the rain which nourishes the earth, and in the sun which sustains life and produces a rich harvest.

To each phase of his creation he gave "a duty which shall not pass away."

St. Paul has a specific mission: "To me, the least of all believers, was given the grace to preach to the Gentiles the unfathomable riches of Christ and to enlighten all men on the mysterious designs which for ages was hidden in God, the Creator of all." (Eph 3:8-9)

Creation's Testimony

Every bud unfolding into a beautiful flower, every scarcely audible peep from a cracked egg releasing new life, every cry of a newborn babe startles us into the realization that our gracious God is sharing life with his creatures.

The massive mountains, the expansive sea, the azure blue sky crescented with a magnificent sunset show forth the beauty of the Lord dimly reflected in his handiwork.

The Lord's creative genius fills us with silent wonder and awe. Then our heart filled to overflowing joyously bursts forth in praise, honor, and glory to the God we dare to call Father.

1 Psalm 19:2-3   Glorious Giant

The heavens declare the glory of God, / and the firmament proclaims his handiwork. / Day pours out the word to day, / and night to night imparts knowledge.

All nature sings the praises of God. The sun, the glorious giant of the heavenly firmament, relects the glory of the Creator. The rhythm of day and night "declare the glory of God."

The power and plan of God in all creation should make our hearts resound with God's glory. Spend the next few moments thanking God for the gift of his life-giving sun as it warms, nourishes, and sustains us here in our earthly exile.

Jesus urges us to listen to his word and be like the saints: "Then the saints will shine like the sun in their Father's kingdom. Let everyone heed what he hears!" (Mt 13:43)

2 Psalm 21:14   Chant His Praise
Be extolled, O Lord, in your strength! / We will sing, chant the praise of your might.

God our Father is omnipotent—all powerful. Nothing is beyond his strength and mighty power. He fashioned our universe. He created our planet earth for our sustenance and survival, but especially for our enjoyment and pleasure.

He built the massive mountains and controls the restless sea. Even a momentary reflection impels us to "sing, chant the praises of his might."

In his vision, John heard every creature say: "To the One seated on the throne, and to the Lamb, / be praise and honor, glory and might, / forever and ever!" (Rev 5:13)

3 Psalm 63:3-4   Master of the Universe
Thus have I gazed toward you in the sanctuary / to see your power and your glory, / For your kindness is a greater good than life; / my lips shall glorify you.

Gazing on the Lord has a great transforming power. We stand in awe and wonder as we gaze on the Lord's might and glory. He is the Creator of the heavens and the world about us. His power fashioned the mountain ranges and controls the mighty oceans. He has power over life and death.

Yet in his great love he stoops down to us. His kindness embraces us, encourages us, energizes us. His kindness fills our hearts with joy. Our lips glorify his name.

With St. Peter we can say: "Master, how good it is for us to be here." (Lk 9:33)

4 Psalm 72:18-19 Glory to God

Blessed be the Lord, the God of Israel, / who alone does wondrous deeds. / And blessed forever be his glorious name; / may the whole earth be filled with his glory. / Amen. Amen.

The love we feel for another, the joy which fills our heart, the excitement of living each new day all reflect the glory of God. Eyes to see, ears to hear, hands to touch, all remind us of him "who alone does wondrous deeds." Let us join the whole world in giving him the glory.

We give glory to God in these inspired words: "To him whose power now at work in us can do immeasurably more than we ask or imagine—to him be glory in the church and in Christ Jesus through all generations, world without end. Amen." (Eph 3:20-21)

5 Psalm 90:16 Seeing God

Let your work be seen by your servants / and your glory by their children.

We often hear the adage "seeing is believing." Thomas earned that unenviable reputation for himself by refusing to believe in the resurrection unless he could see and touch Jesus. Fortunately he saw and believed.

Each day we discover the Lord's work and his glory surrounding us in his ongoing creative work. His providing, sustaining, energizing love envelops us daily. Some reflection on his work and glory will lead us into praising and blessing him.

Jesus is our beacon along the road of life. "I am the light of the world. / No follower of mine shall ever walk in darkness; / no, he shall possess the light of life." (Jn 8:12)

6 **Psalm 102:26-28   Forever**
*Of old you established the earth, / and the heavens
are the work of your hands. / They shall perish, but you
remain . . . / you are the same, and your years have no
end.*

The concept of eternity baffles our mind. We
cannot comprehend a God whose "years have no
end." However, there is much joy and satisfaction
in the thought that we, too, will live forever with
him in the unimaginable bliss of heaven. "Eye has
not seen, ear has not heard, nor has it so much as
dawned on man what God has prepared for those
who love him" (1 Cor 2:9).

This truth makes our lot in life more bearable.
Jesus himself made us a solemn promise: "The
heavens and the earth will pass away but my words
will not pass." (Mt 24:35)

7 **Psalm 113:4-6   Our King**
*High above all nations is the Lord, / above the
heavens is his glory. / Who is like the Lord, our God,
who is enthroned on high / and looks upon the heavens
and the earth below?*

The Lord's attributes are mighty and many. We
cannot possibly comprehend their infinity. He is
Lord of heaven and earth. He is the Creator and
sustainer of the immense universe calling each star
by name.

He is also a God present to us, abiding with us
and in us. He knows our every concern and is
present to support and encourage us. He remains
with us above all to let us know how much he loves
us. Little wonder that we want to burst forth with
enthusiastic praise of our Lord and God.

Jesus declared his kingship before Pilate: "My
kingdom does not belong to this world. . . . As it is,
my kingdom is not here." (Jn 18:36)

Part III

Your Heavenly Father Knows All That You Need.

(Mt 6:32)

Providential Love

God's love for every one of us is absolutely infinite. One of the many dimensions of the Father's love is his providential care and concern for us at every moment of the day.

How briefly, yet how powerfully Jesus explained the loving providence of the Father when he said: "Look at the birds in the sky. They do not sow or reap, they gather nothing into barns; yet your heavenly Father feeds them."

Then he makes a point when he asks: "Are not you more important than they?" And again: "Your heavenly Father knows all that you need" (Mt 6:26f). An awareness of so great a love leaves no room for worry or anxiety.

1 Psalm 3:6 Safe in God's Keeping
When I lie down in sleep, / I wake again, for the Lord sustains me.

We have no need for sleeping pills or tranquilizers, nor will we experience insomnia, when we know that God surrounds us with his loving protection.

Peaceful sleep is God's gift to us. During sleep our tired body and mind recuperate to begin a new day renewed and refreshed. When we awaken, our first thought should be an act of thanksgiving by offering God our whole day in return for his loving care.

The sacred writer reminds us: "The fear of the Lord is an aid to life; / one eats and sleeps without being visited / by misfortune." (Prv 19:23)

2 Psalm 36:6-7   Love Unlimited

O Lord, your kindness reaches to heaven; / your faithfulness, to the clouds. / Your justice is like the mountains of God; / your judgments, like the mighty deep; / man and beast you save, O Lord.

In picturesque language the psalmist portrays the kindness and the faithfulness of God by comparing God's goodness to the immensity of the mountains and the depths of the sea. Even these metaphors cannot encompass the unfathomable, limitless love which God has for us.

God is eternal and immutable. His love is just as great today as always. All he asks of us is to let him love us, to be open to receive his gifts.

The beloved disciple explains it in these words: "God's love was revealed in our midst in this way: / he sent his only Son to the world / that we might have life through him." (1 Jn 4:9)

3 Psalm 36:8-9   No More Thirst

How precious is your kindness, O God! / The children of men take refuge in the shadow of your wings. / They have their fill of the prime gifts of your house; / from your delightful stream you give them to drink.

The bounty of God's prime gifts to us is compared to a delightful stream of refreshing water. Water is essential to life.

Jesus often used the image of living water to signify the divine life which he shares with us. The living water of Jesus' divine life is essential for our eternal salvation.

Jesus himself best describes its potential: "Whoever drinks the water I give him / will never be thirsty; / no, the water I give / shall become a fountain within him, / leaping up to provide eternal life." (Jn 4:14)

4 Psalm 36:10-11 Light and Life

For with you is the fountain of life, / and in your light we see light. / Keep up your kindness toward your friends, / your just defense of the upright of heart.

Light in scriptural language signifies the presence of God. Light is also symbolic of his goodness which is the source of our happiness.

In the light of God's presence we can see more clearly how we fit into the jigsaw puzzle of life. We must fulfill our role, otherwise the picture will never be complete.

When we cannot see the pattern of life, we beg God in his goodness and kindness to guide us.

Jesus made this thought quite clear when he said: "I am the light of the world. / No follower of mine shall ever walk in darkness; / no, he shall possess the light of life." (Jn 8:12)

5 Psalm 67:7 Bountiful Harvest

The earth has yielded its fruits; / God, our God, has blessed us. / May God bless us, / and may all the ends of the earth fear him!

Harvest time is that season which reminds us very forcefully of God's divine providence. The golden grain of the fields, the luscious fruit of the trees and vines as well as the abundance of nourishing vegetables all manifest the goodness of God.

The warm sunshine, the rich soil, and the life-giving rain are all blessings which our provident Father showers upon us.

Harvest time stirs our heart to a genuine spirit of gratitude.

Jesus taught us to be grateful by his own example: "Jesus then took the loaves of bread, gave thanks, and passed them around to those reclining there." (Jn 6:11)

6 Psalm 68:10-11   Providential Love

A bountiful rain you showered down, O God, / upon your inheritance; / you restored the land when it languished; / Your flock settled in it; / in your goodness, O God, you provided it for the needy.

With these pastoral images the psalmist tries to verbalize his appreciation of the overwhelming providential love of God for us.

We are his inheritance. His solicitude for our spiritual welfare is even greater. He gives us every grace and blessing we need to reach our home with him.

How encouraging is Jesus' reminder to us: "If God can clothe in such splendor the grass of the field, which blooms today and is thrown on the fire tomorrow, will he not provide much more for you, O weak in faith!" (Mt 6:30)

7 Psalm 81:17   Superabundance

While Israel I would feed with the best of wheat, / and with honey from the rock.

God rewarded the faithful people of Israel by feeding them "with the best of wheat and with honey from the rock." Honey from the rock is a Hebrew expression meaning an extreme abundance.

We are the new Israel. God's loving care and concern for us will provide us with a superabundance of everything we need if we are faithful to him. He asks us to trust him and walk in his ways.

St. Paul tells us God's generosity is immeasurable: "It is in Christ and through his blood that we have been redeemed and our sins forgiven, so immeasurably generous is God's favor to us." (Eph 1:7f)

I Will Pasture My Sheep

Throughout sacred Scripture we find the image of the Good Shepherd used to remind us of God's loving providence, nurturing, protecting, and providing for us without interruption.

With every respiration, we breath in God-given oxygen to sustain and energize us. Every step we take is granted to guide us in our daily work. Every morsel of food is another proof of our Father's providential love.

May this week be a grateful, loving response to so gracious and generous a Father.

1 Psalm 23:1-2   Restful Waters

The Lord is my shepherd; I shall not want. / In verdant pastures he gives me repose; / Beside restful waters he leads me; / he refreshes my soul.

Jesus refers to his dwelling within us as "living water." The restful waters to which he leads us is the quiet joy and interior peace of his abiding presence.

We are his sheep. As our Shepherd, he knows that sheep are fearful of rapid-running water; hence he nurtures us in the quiet, prayerful solitude of our own heart.

Jesus assures us that he alone can satisfy our thirst: "But whoever drinks the water I give him / will never be thirsty; / no, the water I give / shall become a fountain within him, / leaping up to provide eternal life." (Jn 4:14)

2 Psalm 23:3-4   Rod and Staff
He guides me in right paths / for his name's sake. / Even though I walk in the dark valley / I fear no evil; for you are at my side / With your rod and your staff / that give me courage.

As the Good Shepherd, the Lord's provident, protective love envelops us at every moment. A shepherd guides his sheep along safe paths with his staff and defends them from harm with his rod.

This figure portrays the Lord's loving care and concern for each one of us. When we recognize him as our Good Shepherd, we will seek the shelter of his love. "I am the good shepherd. / I know my sheep / and my sheep know me ... / for these sheep I will give my life." (Jn 10:14f)

3 Psalm 23:6   Fullness of Life
Only goodness and kindness follow me / all the days of my life; / And I shall dwell in the house of the Lord / for years to come.

In his goodness and kindness, Jesus, our Good Shepherd, rescued us from condemnation by his redeeming love and showed us the path through the dark valley of our earthly exile into our heavenly home.

His goodness and kindness leads us to the fullness of life so that we can "dwell in the house of the Lord." Jesus tells us that this is precisely why he came: "I came that they might have life / and have it to the full." (Jn 10:10)

4 Psalm 65:12-13   Poetry in Plenty

You have crowned the year with your bounty, / and your paths overflow with a rich harvest; / The untilled meadows overflow with it, / and rejoicing clothes the hills.

This pastoral image poetically portrays God's goodness in providing us with a rich harvest as he crowns each year with his bounty.

The overflowing abundance of the untilled meadows reminds us that while God expects our cooperation and industry, he alone can give the increase.

St. Paul's statement is so accurate: "I planted the seed and Apollos watered it, but God made it grow. This means that neither he who plants nor he who waters is of any special account, only God, who gives the growth." (1 Cor 3:6f)

5 Psalm 65:14   Growing Spiritually

The fields are garmented with flocks / and the valleys blanketed with grain. / They shout and sing for joy.

A leisurely drive through the country will make us want to "shout and sing for joy." As we contemplate the growing grain and produce, the well-fed flocks and herds, the abundance of life-giving water, we come to realize once again how profound is God's providential love which is being poured out upon us in torrents night and day.

Jesus gave us a splendid illustration in comparing our spiritual growth with God's grace to a natural growth of seed. He said: "This is how it is with the reign of God. A man scatters seed on the ground. He goes to bed and gets up day after day. Through it all the seed sprouts and grows without his knowing how it happens." (Mk 4:26-27)

6 Psalm 90:17   Gracious Care
May the gracious care of the Lord our God be ours; / prosper the work of our hands for us!

God has called each one of us to a special vocation and a particular ministry. We could never succeed in fulfilling the duties of every day without the Lord's special help.

In his gracious care the Lord inspires and motivates us. He enlightens and guides us. He nurtures and strengthens us. With the assistance of his providential love, the work of our hands will prosper.

The Lord awaits our asking for his gracious care.

Jesus cautions us about needing his help: "No more than a branch can bear fruit of itself / apart from the vine, / can you bear fruit / apart from me." (Jn 15:4)

7 Psalm 111:5   None Greater
He has given food to those who fear him; / he will forever be mindful of his covenant.

The Lord faithfully provided food for the Israelites in the desert because he was ever mindful of the covenant he had made with them. In the liturgy of the church, the manna was always considered a type, or figure of the Eucharist.

Jesus promised us the bread of heaven; he prepared us for it and, true to his covenant, he gave us himself in the Eucharist as his farewell gift to us.

St. Paul reminds us that we must also be true to the covenant: "Every time, then, you eat this bread and drink this cup, you proclaim the death of the Lord until he comes!" (1 Cor 11:26)

Who Does God Save?

God wants to save us more than we could want it ourselves. His two conditions are: 1.) certain standards of living and 2.) a real desire on our part to be saved.

In the Beatitudes Jesus set forth standards for Christian living. He developed and synthesized the norms of living which would lead us to salvation. He promised a blessing for each one of these norms.

Secondly, Jesus wants us to realize that salvation is his gift to us. He also wants us to recognize our own helplessness and to call to him to save us.

St. Paul reminds us: "I repeat, it is owing to his favor that salvation is yours through faith. This is not your own doing, it is God's gift; neither is it a reward for anything you have accomplished . . ." (Eph 2:8-9).

1 Psalm 116:6-7   Humble of Heart

The Lord keeps the little ones; / I was brought low, and he saved me. / Return, O my soul, to your tranquillity, / for the Lord has been good to you.

"Little ones" in Scripture does not refer to physical age but rather to those who are meek and humble of heart, those who are receptive to the influence of God's grace.

When we recognize that of ourselves we can do nothing and acknowledge that the Lord has been good to us, then we are on the way to salvation. Jesus assures us that the lowly will enter heaven: "I assure you, unless you change and become like little children, you will not enter the kingdom of God." (Mt 18:3)

2 Psalm 34:7 Sanctifying Suffering
When the afflicted man called out, the Lord heard, / and from all his distress he saved him.

Suffering and sorrow is the lot of every one of us. We may not understand the reason for it. We may even rebel against it. Such a reaction is only human.

When we ask the Lord's help in our affliction, we can more easily bear our cross. We will also experience great peace. We may even recognize it as a giant step toward our salvation.

To the sorrowing, Jesus promised eternal consolation: "Blest too are the sorrowing; they shall be consoled." (Mt 5:4)

3 Psalm 18:28-29 Gentle and Humble
For lowly people you save / but haughty eyes you bring low; / You indeed, O Lord, give light to my lamp; / O my God, you brighten the darkness about me.

Jesus always had high praise for the lowly. Scripture calls them the *anawim*. They are the humble, gentle, unsophisticated, happy people who are open and eager to hear the word of God.

The lowly come very close in their relationship with the Lord, who then becomes a light in the darkness for them. We can become lowly when we strive to learn from Jesus who was gentle and humble of heart. The Lord will then brighten the dark moments for us on our way to heaven.

Jesus singled out the lowly as being especially blessed: "Blest are the lowly; they shall inherit the land." (Mt 5:5)

4 Psalm 145:19   Fear But No Fear
He fulfills the desire of those who fear him, / he hears their cry and saves them.

When Scripture uses the word "fear," it does not denote the emotion of anxious concern nor a dread of some lurking danger. Rather, fear means a profound reverence and respect for God's might and power. When we say that we fear God, it means that we stand in awe and admiration of the overflowing love and the abundant goodness which our gracious God continues to pour out upon us.

When we reverence God in this fashion, he will fulfill our every desire, especially the longing we have to be with him for all eternity.

Jesus assures us this reverence will be blessed: "Blest are they who hunger and thirst for holiness; / they shall have their fill." (Mt 5:6)

5 Psalm 7:11-12   Primary Priority
A shield before me is God, / who saves the upright of heart; / A just judge is God, / a God who punishes day by day.

To live a good and holy life we must be single-minded in doing the will of God at all times. Many around us would try to dissuade us from the road we have chosen and to abandon the standards we have set as our goal. We must dare to be different.

Jesus gives us the example. He broke with the culture of his day because he had only one principal concern, and that was to do the will of his Father at all times.

Jesus tells us how happy we will be when we make the will of God our first priority. It is a sure path to salvation. "Blest are the single-hearted for they shall see God." (Mt 5:8)

6 Psalm 34:15-16 Path to Peace

Turn from evil, and do good; / seek peace, and follow after it. / The Lord has eyes for the just, / and ears for their cry.

Jesus invites us to follow him and become his disciples. We must strive to have the mind and heart of Jesus. The psalmist tells us how to begin this transformation: "Turn from evil, and do good."

He also encourages us to "seek peace, and follow after it." True peace flows from our personal relationship with the Lord. When we enjoy genuine peace, it naturally radiates through us to others. Then we become peacemakers.

Jesus pronounced a blessing for peacemakers: "Blest too the peacemakers; they shall be called sons of God." (Mt 5:9)

7 Psalm 55:17-18 Persecution a Paradox

But I will call upon God, / and the Lord will save me. / In the evening, and at dawn, and at noon, / I will grieve and moan, / and he will hear my voice.

The joys and the happy moments of life are mingled with difficulties strewn along our path. We meet them morning, noon, and evening. We should not be surprised at their occurrence since Jesus already prepared us for them.

Jesus warned us that the road might be steep and rocky, the door narrow, and the cross heavy. He also told us that he would be with us pulling his share of the yoke which would make our yoke easy and our burden light.

St. James encourages us never to lose hope but to trust that every trial contributes to our glory. "Happy the man who holds out to the end through trial! Once he has been proved, he will receive the crown of life the Lord has promised to those who love him." (Jas 1:12)

Boundless Munificence

We are spoiled children. What necessity do we really lack in life? Visualize our provident Father asking you what more should he have given you that he has not already given. The question may startle us into a realization of his boundless goodness to us.

Words and expressions of thanks do not quite convey our deep sense of appreciation. A hymn of praise to our benevolent Father for his infinite goodness seems to express more accurately our heartfelt thanks and gratitude.

May praise be ever on our lips!

1 Psalm 7:18   King of Glory
I will give thanks to the Lord for his justice, / and sing praise to the name of the Lord Most High.

God heard the prayer of the psalmist and protected him from his enemies. In gratitude, he was loud in his praise of God's holiness.

The "Lord Most High" surrounds us with his protective love especially against all the machinations of the devil. We are not even aware of the countless occasions when the Lord has rescued us from spiritual and physical harm. We praise him particularly for his justice, his divine life, which he communicates to us through the power of Christ's resurrection.

St. Paul's teaching brings joy to our heart: ". . . just as Christ was raised from the dead by the glory of the Father, we too might live a new life. If we have been united with him through likeness to his death, so shall we be through a like resurrection." (Rom 6:4-5)

2 Psalm 9:2-3 Joyous Praise

I will give thanks to you, O Lord, with all my heart; / I will declare all your wondrous deeds. / I will be glad and exult in you; / I will sing praise to your name, Most High.

Today set aside some time for quiet and solitude to recall the wondrous deeds of the Lord in your life. As we recall the outpouring of his gifts and blessings, our minds stagger in wonder while our hearts want to burst forth in joyous gratitude.

The psalmist's words are a fitting expression of gratitude and praise. Let our prayer of praise rise from the very depth of our being as we ring out our song of praise.

Jesus knows that this time is essential; hence he invites us: "Come by yourselves to an out-of-the-way place and rest a little." (Mk 6:31)

3 Psalm 57:8 Never Wavering

My heart is steadfast, O God; my heart is steadfast; / I will sing and chant praise.

After pleading with God for help in his need, the sacred writer turns to God with this joyful expression of trust.

When we ponder the tremendous love of the Lord for us and when we recall how frequently he has responded to our every need, our hearts too are steadfast. When we reflect that our confidence and trust in the Lord has never been in vain, our steadfast hearts sing and chant his praise.

St. Paul in his pastoral concern says: "Finally, my brothers, your thoughts should be wholly directed to all that is true, all that deserves respect, all that is honest, pure, admirable, decent, virtuous, or worthy of praise." (Phil 4:8)

4 Psalm 67:5-6
Praise Everywhere and Always

May the nations be glad and exult / because you rule the peoples in equity; / the nations on the earth you guide. / May the peoples praise you, O God; / may all the peoples praise you!

This is a prayer pleading that all nations may recognize the blessings of the Lord as he governs wisely, rules over the seasons, and provides an abundant harvest for our sustenance, not to mention the other gifts he daily rains down on us.

As we ponder God's goodness, we too desire that all peoples glorify him for his loving concern. What more appropriate prayer can we offer than: "May all the peoples praise you!"

St. Paul's words are eloquent: "He is the pledge of our inheritance, the first payment against the full redemption of a people God has made his own, to praise his glory." (Eph 1:14)

5 Psalm 71:8 and 14   Day By Day
My mouth shall be filled with your praise, / with your glory day by day . . . . / But I will always hope / and praise you ever more and more.

The edifice of our spiritual life can be compared to the construction of a building. It is constructed brick by brick, day by day.

Giving God glory day by day is a growth process. Praising and glorifying the Lord daily keeps our attention riveted on him. With the Lord as our goal, the daily burdens and anxieties become more peripheral. We will always hope because we know that God is always faithful to his promises.

St. Paul explains the reason for our hope: "We were predestined to praise his glory by being the first to hope in Christ." (Eph 1:11b-12)

6 Psalm 79:13   No Greater Shepherd
Then we, your people and the sheep of your pasture, / will give thanks to you forever; / through all generations we will declare your praise.

The image of the Lord as Shepherd and us as "the sheep of his pasture" bespeaks the loving care and concern that the Lord has for us. He guides and leads us along life's pathway toward our heavenly goal.

In return for such goodness, all we can do is thank and praise him all the days of our life.

What joy Jesus brings us when he says: "I am the good shepherd; / the good shepherd lays down his life for the sheep." (Jn 10:11)

7 Psalm 145:3-4   God's Might and Power
Great is the Lord and highly to be praised; / his greatness is unsearchable. / Generation after generation praises your works / and proclaims your might.

The might and power of God is certainly unsearchable. His power is concealed in all his creation from the tiny atom to the mighty sun.

As we stand in awe and reverence, our heart longs to sing his praises. We join with all peoples in praising and glorifying his mighty power.

Overwhelmed by the mystery of God, the inspired writer exclaimed: "How deep are the riches and the wisdom and the knowledge of God! How inscrutable his judgments, how unsearchable his ways!" (Rom 11:33)

Part IV

As Your Father Is Compassionate

(Lk 6:36)

Our Compassionate Father

One of the mysterious attributes of God is his inexhaustible mercy. God wants to forgive, heal, and redeem us more than we could want it ourselves. Such an unquenchable love baffles our minds.

God himself reveals this love when he says: "It is I, I, who wipe out, / for my own sake, your offenses; / your sins I remember no more." (Is 43:25)

Psalm 103 is a hymn of thanksgiving, praising God for his magnificent mercy and compassionate love.

Throughout this week, we will reflect on various aspects of God's generous and gracious love as expressed in this psalm.

1 Psalm 103:1-2   Sing His Praises

Bless the Lord, O my soul; / and all my being, bless his holy name. / Bless the Lord, O my soul, / and forget not all his benefits.

Every Christian who experiences God's loving mercy and compassion is a happy person. Even though the Lord is the transcendent God of heaven and earth, he still abides with us to forgive, heal, and redeem us.

Our gratitude for such great mercy naturally leads us into a hymn of praise for all his benefits. "All this is the work of the kindness of our God; / he, the Dayspring, shall visit us in his mercy." (Lk 1:78)

2 Psalm 103:3-4   Healer-Redeemer
He pardons all your iniquities, / he heals all your ills. / He redeems your life from destruction, / he crowns you with kindness and compassion.

Jesus became incarnate in our world in order to forgive our sinfulness, to heal us in every area of our brokenness. He took on our human nature with all its physical, intellectual, and psychological limitations so that he might redeem us and give us the capacity to receive his divine life dwelling within us.

Jesus himself affirmed his mission: "I have come to call sinners, not the self-righteous." (Mk 2:17)

3 Psalm 103:8-9   Incomprehensible Mercy
Merciful and gracious is the Lord, / slow to anger and abounding in kindness. / He will not always chide, / nor does he keep his wrath forever.

Do we have the courage to ponder our own sinfulness, our frequent rejection of God's love, and still listen to him telling us that he loves anyway? Such a love is beyond our comprehension.

All that the Lord asks is a humble acknowledgment of our sinfulness and a penitent disposition to receive his mercy and forgiveness.

May Jesus say of us as he did of the penitent woman: "I tell you, that is why her many sins are forgiven—because of her great love. Little is forgiven the one whose love is small." (Lk 7:47)

4 Psalm 103:10   Paradox of Mercy

Not according to our sins does he deal with us, / nor does he requite us according to our crimes.

Many of us have the notion that God portions out his mercy and forgiveness as we merit it or earn it. God's mercy does not depend upon our deserving it, only on our willingness to receive his loving forgiveness.

The paradox is: God's grace is greater than man's sin.

St. Paul reminds us also: "Despite the increase of sin, grace has far surpassed it, so that, as sin reigned through death, grace may reign by way of justice leading to eternal life, through Jesus Christ our Lord." (Rom 5:20-21)

5 Psalm 103:11-12   Mercy Unlimited

For as the heavens are high above the earth, / so surpassing is his kindness toward those who fear him. / As far as the east is from the west, / so far has he put our transgressions from us.

In picturesque language the psalmist tries to convince us of the immensity of God's mercy and compassion by comparing it to the infinite distance between earth and heaven.

Similarly, from east to west is a continuous circle without beginning or end. Such is God's loving forgiveness. It is limitless, unending, always present.

Sacred Scripture reassures us: "We have this confidence in God: that he hears us whenever we ask for anything according to his will. And since we know that he hears us whenever we ask, we know that what we have asked him for is ours." (1 Jn 5:14-15)

6 Psalm 103:13-14 So Gracious a Father
As a father has compassion on his children, / so the Lord has compassion on those who fear him. / For he knows how we are formed, / he remembers that we are dust.

What an apt comparison! A father's love for his children forgives their faults and failings because he understands their self-will and selfishness.

Our heavenly Father is eager to forgive us because he knows our humanness, our brokenness. He also remembers that we are dust.

Jesus tells us: "If you, with all your sins, know how to give your children what is good, how much more will your heavenly Father give good things to anyone who asks him!" (Mt 7:11)

7 Psalm 103:20-21 Worthy of Praise
Bless the Lord, all you his angels, / you mighty in strength, who do his bidding / obeying his spoken word. / Bless the Lord, all you his hosts, / his ministers, who do his will.

When we ponder God's forgiving, healing, redeeming love for us regardless of what we have done, we are completely overwhelmed. Words cannot possibly convey our feelings of grateful love and praise.

With the psalmist, let us call upon all the hosts of heaven to praise and glorify our merciful God in our name.

With the heavenly choir let us sing: "Worthy is the Lamb that was slain / to receive power and riches, wisdom and strength, / honor and glory and praise!" (Rev 5:12)

Prayer of Repentance

Psalm 51 is a powerful prayer for obtaining the Lord's forgiveness and healing. As we pray this psalm, we can stand before God guilty but unafraid. As we make this prayer of David our own, we are disposing ourselves to receive an abundance of our loving Father's mercy and compassion.

1 Psalm 51:3-4
The Lord's Merciful Goodness

Have mercy on me, O God, in your goodness; / in the greatness of your compassion wipe out my offense. / Thoroughly wash me from my guilt / and of my sin cleanse me.

Jesus came into the world as our Savior and Redeemer. As we appeal to his mercy and compassion, Jesus is pleased because we are acknowledging him for what he wants to be most—Redeemer and healer.

Our attitude also bespeaks our openness to the transformation he wants to effect within us.

With the tax collector, let us pray: "O God, be merciful to me, a sinner." (Lk 18:13)

2 **Psalm 51:5-6   I, Too, Am a Sinner**
*For I acknowledge my offense, / and my sin is before
me always: / "Against you only have I sinned, / and
done what is evil in your sight."*

A deep sense of sin and a humble acknowledgement of our waywardness is the first all-important
step toward reconciliation with our loving Father.

Such an attitude will unleash the floodgates of
his divine mercy and compassion.

With the prodigal son we confess: "Father, I
have sinned against God and against you; I no
longer deserve to be called your son." (Lk 15:21)

3 **Psalm 51:9-10   Source of Joy**
*Cleanse me of sin with hyssop, that I may be
purified; / wash me, and I shall be whiter than snow. /
Let me hear the sounds of joy and gladness.*

The Old Testament psalmist begged for the
purifying rite with hyssop, but Jesus has given us a
more powerful sign of purification.

The words of absolution in the sacrament of
penance can well be "the sounds of joy and
gladness" which we, as well as the psalmist, long to
hear.

Jesus instituted the sacrament of penance when
he said: "Receive the Holy Spirit. / If you forgive
men's sins, / they are forgiven them; / if you hold
them bound, / they are held bound." (Jn 20:
22-23)

4 Psalm 51:12-13 Sanctifying Spirit
A clean heart create for me, O God, / and a steadfast spirit renew within me. / Cast me not out from your presence, / and your holy spirit take not from me.

The psalmist did not understand clearly the "holy spirit" for whom he prayed. Jesus revealed the Holy Spirit as the sanctifying, purifying Spirit who would continue his redemptive work in us. We, too, pray: Come, Holy Spirit.

Long ago the Father promised us his purifying Spirit: "I will put my Spirit within you and make you live by my statutes, careful to observe my decrees." (Ez 36:27)

5 Psalm 51:14 Redeeming Love
Give me back the joy of your salvation, / and a willing spirit sustain in me.

God's forgiving love is a mystery. He loves us so much, he wants to forgive us more than we could even want forgiveness. That kind of love we cannot fathom.

We can almost hear God say: "I don't care what you have done; I love you anyway."

Jesus' words to the criminal on the cross could also be addressed to us if our disposition is the same as his: "I assure you: this day you will be with me in paradise." (Lk 23:43)

6 Psalm 51:15 Be Radiant
I will teach transgressors your ways, / and sinners shall return to you.

The quiet, interior peace which we experience in knowing that the Lord loves us with a forgiving, healing, redeeming love will reflect itself in all our actions and attitudes.

This radiant peace will encourage others to find their way back into the embrace of the Father's merciful compassion.

St. James's words are encouraging: "Remember this: the person who brings a sinner back from his way will save his soul from death and cancel a multitude of sins." (Jas 5:20)

7 Psalm 51:19 A Contrite Heart
My sacrifice, O God, is a contrite spirit; / a heart contrite and humbled, O God, you will not spurn.

Our interior disposition is of paramount importance if we wish to obtain God's forgiveness. Humility is essential in forming a contrite heart.

A contrite spirit melts the heart of God who wishes not the death of a sinner, but that he be converted and live.

Jesus set Simon, the Pharisee, straight when he said: "I tell you, that is why her many sins are forgiven—because of her great love. Little is forgiven the one whose love is small." (Lk 7:47)

Mercy I Desire

In Semitic parlance, mercy has a whole spectrum of meanings: tenderness, pity, compassion, clemency, goodness, love. In Scripture, the word mercy is often used when speaking of God's forgiving and pardoning of offenses.

For the Hebrew, the manifestation of God's tenderness is occasioned by human misery, especially man's need for forgiveness. It also implies that man, in turn, ought to show mercy to his neighbor in imitation of his Creator.

Sirach capsulizes this whole idea when he says: "Compassionate and merciful is the Lord; / he forgives sins, he saves in time of trouble." (Sir 2:11)

1 Psalm 34:23   On to Glory
But the Lord redeems the lives of his servants; / no one incurs guilt who takes refuge in him.

In his great compassion the Father gave us his Son to redeem us. In turn, Jesus' love is so immense that he willingly laid down his life for us.

Salvation is God's gift to us. We cannot merit it. We cannot earn it. It is not a reward but a gift. We need to be open and receptive to this unique gift.

St. Paul expresses this truth in these words: "God is rich in mercy; because of his great love for us he brought us to life with Christ when we were dead in sin. By this favor you were saved." (Eph 2:4-5)

2 Psalm 69:17 Bounteous Mercy
Answer me, O Lord, for bounteous is your kindness; / in your great mercy turn toward me.

Like the psalmist, we have experienced the bounteous mercy of God all the days of our life. His mercy and compassion is ever present if we humbly and sincerely acknowledge our sinfulness and strive earnestly to make our offenses few.

Our prayer for forgiveness will always melt the heart of our compassionate Father, for his mercy endures forever. We can be certain that when we pray for forgiveness, our petition will reach the throne of mercy.

May our prayer always be the same as the man in the temple: "O God, be merciful to me, a sinner." (Lk 18:13)

3 Psalm 79:8 Our Heritage
Remember not against us the iniquities of the past; / may your compassion quickly come to us, / for we are brought very low.

As we experience in our own life the effects of the sins of our forefathers—*e.g.* lack of peace, injustice, hatred, and prejudice—so our sins also will influence future generations.

We beg our Father in his mercy and compassion to forgive and heal these effects of sin and grant to us and our children genuine joy, peace, and happiness in his presence. "You continue your kindness through a thousand generations; and you repay the fathers' guilt, even into the lap of their sons who follow them." (Jer 32:18)

4 **Psalm 79:9   Prayer for Forgiveness**
Help us, O God our savior, / because of the glory of your name; / Deliver us and pardon our sins / for your name's sake.

Our God is a forgiving God. His boundless mercy and compassion reveals the infinite dimension of his forgiving, healing, redeeming love.

The manifestation of his love fills our heart with sorrow and gratitude and impels us to honor and glorify his holy name.

The Lord himself tells us how compelling is his love: "It is I, I, who wipe out, / for my own sake, your offenses; / your sins I remember no more." (Is 43:25)

5 **Psalm 86:15   Pardon and Peace**
You, O Lord, are a God merciful and gracious, / slow to anger, abounding in kindness and fidelity.

When we experience the Lord's forgiving, healing love, we enjoy a peace which will move us to glorify and praise him with greater fervor than ever. As we become more aware of his mercy and compassion, we will want his forgiving love to become better known and appreciated.

Radiating the peace and joy of our hearts will encourage sinners to seek his pardon and peace. This is also a part of our mission in life.

St. James encourages us in this apostolate when he says: "Remember this: the person who brings a sinner back from his way will save his soul from death and cancel a multitude of sins." (Jas 5:20)

6 Psalm 136:1   His Mercy Endures Forever
Give thanks to the Lord, for he is good, / for his mercy endures forever.

The refrain "his mercy endures forever" occurs many times in the psalms—twenty-six times in this psalm alone. It reminds us of an oft-repeated response of a litany. Its repetition is necessary since we fall frequently in spite of our best resolves. We need to know that God's merciful forgiveness is always reaching out to us regardless of our many infidelities.

We cannot comprehend so great a compassionate love. All we can do is "give thanks to the Lord, for he is good."

How comforting are the words of Jesus: "I tell you, there will likewise be more joy in heaven over one repentant sinner than over ninety-nine righteous people who have no need to repent." (Lk 15:7)

7 Psalm 145:8-9   Easy Return
The Lord is gracious and merciful, / slow to anger and of great kindness. / The Lord is good to all / and compassionate toward all his works.

We are all familiar with the exit signs along our freeways, inviting us to stop to refresh ourselves and to refuel our vehicles. We find similar signs along our highway to heaven which would lure us away from the Lord, our final destination.

If we should succumb to such a temptation and take an exit diverting us away from the Lord, we can be certain that in his great mercy, he will lead us back to the safe and narrow road.

In God's word we are assured: "So let us confidently approach the throne of grace to receive mercy and favor and to find help in time of need." (Heb 4:16)

Mystery of Love

The mystery of God's love baffles us beyond comprehension. His love is so great that he wants to forgive and heal us more than we could want it ourselves. He himself said that his love compels him to forgive: "It is I, I, who wipe out, / for my own sake, your offenses; / your sins I remember no more." (Is 43:25)

Jesus' statement is even more amazing: "I tell you, there will likewise be more joy in heaven over one repentant sinner than over ninety-nine righteous people who have no need to repent." (Lk 15:7)

For such an overwhelming love, let us praise and thank the Lord.

1 Psalm 18:4   Divine Deliverer
Praised be the Lord, I exclaim, / and I am safe from my enemies.

In the opening verses the writer uses many terms in an attempt to describe the powerful protection which God has been for him. He calls God "my strength, my fortress, my deliverer, my rock of refuge, my stronghold, the horn of my salvation."

When we contemplate the countless times God has shielded and protected us from spiritual and physical danger, we too will find ourselves groping for expressions to describe God's fidelity.

St. Paul reveals God's protective power as he relates his own transformation from foe to friend: "They had only heard that 'he who was formerly persecuting us is now preaching the faith he tried to destroy,' and they gave glory to God on my account." (Gal 1:23-24)

2 Psalm 22:27 *Anawim*
The lowly shall eat their fill; / they who seek the Lord shall praise him: /"May your hearts be ever merry!"

In the Beatitudes, Jesus called the lowly blessed. "Blest are the lowly, they shall inherit the land," meaning heaven.

By the lowly, Scripture means those persons who are receptive to God's word. It also includes those who are not bound by all sorts of material attachments and who are able to keep their focus on the Lord, giving him the proper priority.

Our Blessed Mother was such a person. She could say: "My being proclaims the greatness of the Lord, / my spirit finds joy in God my savior, / For he has looked upon his servant in her lowliness." (Lk 1:46f)

3 Psalm 27:6 Love Sings
Even now my head is held high / above my enemies on every side. / And I will offer in his tent / sacrifices with shouts of gladness; / I will sing and chant praise to the Lord.

The most comforting and consoling truth in our spiritual journey is the awareness that we are loved and cherished by God. This heart knowledge gives us courage and strength in the face of all that confronts us along life's pathway.

Like the psalmist, nothing will disturb us or cause us to be frightened or afraid because we are protected and shielded by God's love for us personally and individually. With joyous hearts we sing the praises of the Lord.

Jesus assures us: "The Father already loves you, / because you have loved me / and have believed that I came from God." (Jn 16:27)

4 Psalm 34:2-4 With Your Whole Being
I will bless the Lord at all times; / his praise shall be ever in my mouth. / Let my soul glory in the Lord; / the lowly will hear me and be glad. / Glorify the Lord with me, / let us together extol his name.

In these words we remind ourselves to bless and glorify God for his caring and concerned love for us which protects and provides for us at all times.

Praising God with our soul means with our whole being—mind, heart, lips—our whole person. By our words, actions, and attitudes, we are inviting others to join us that together we may extol his name. Thus the glory of God swells into a great crescendo.

Jesus' statement is brief but requires a lifetime of living: "You shall love the Lord your God / with your whole heart, / with your whole soul, / and with all your mind." (Mt 22:37)

5 Psalm 74:21 Learn from Me
May the humble not retire in confusion; / may the afflicted and the poor praise your name.

In these few words we are asking that the humble and the afflicted may continue to praise God. It may be difficult for them to see the will of God in their lives. In fact, they may become discouraged and confused. However, if they persevere in praising God, they will maintain their peace.

There is an important lesson here. Keeping our sights fixed on God and praising him for his goodness will make us a happy, joyful disciple.

Jesus prepares us for what will happen in our lives: "You will weep and mourn / while the world rejoices; / you will grieve for a time, / but your grief will be turned into joy." (Jn 16:20)

6 Psalm 102:19-20   Manifold Mercy

Let this be written for the generation to come, / and let his future creatures praise the Lord: / "The Lord looked down from his holy height, / from heaven he beheld the earth. . . ."

This fifth penitential psalm recounts God's great mercy and compassion as he "looked down from his holy height" and "beheld the earth." Mankind severed its relationship with God through its sinfulness. The human race was helpless, miserable, desolate.

Our merciful Father gave us a Redeemer in the person of Jesus. His redeeming love brought hope, forgiveness, peace, and joy to all our hearts. May we and all future generations praise the Lord for his unfathomable love.

Jesus was happy to tell us: "The Father loves me for this: / that I lay down my life / to take it up again." (Jn 10:17)

7 Psalm 115:1   Not to Us

Not to us, O Lord, not to us / but to your name give glory / because of your kindness, because of your truth.

How apt is this prayer! We are often beset by megalomania. We want everything to happen according to our wishes and plans. We feel so indispensable at times. We may be convinced that our opinions and our input is vitally important to the success of any project.

We may be momentarily oblivious of the fact that every thought and inspiration, every skill and facility, are gifts from God. How much we need to pray: "Not to us, O Lord, not to us."

The writer of Hebrews put it this way: "Every house is founded by someone, but God is the founder of all." (Heb 3:4)

Part V

Come to Me.
(Mt 11:28)

God's Saving Presence in Our Distress

We are pilgrims on our way to the Father. We must cross over stormy seas and through the desert. We struggle with our sinfulness.

But in his bountiful love, God rescues us from any danger which may threaten. Jesus promised that he would never leave us orphans, but that he and the Father would make their dwelling place with us.

During this week let us prayerfully recall some of the Lord's goodness. The psalmist reminds us four different times how we should respond: "Let them give thanks to the Lord for his kindness / and his wondrous deeds to the children of men." (Ps 107:8, 15, 21, 31)

1 Psalm 107:1 Give Thanks
Give thanks to the Lord, for he is good, / for his kindness endures forever!

These words are an urgent invitation to thank God for his inexhaustible love, especially that love which always comes to our rescue in distress.

Pray the first line yourself: "Give thanks to the Lord for he is good." Hear yourself or another respond: "for his kindness endures forever." Today thank the Lord for being our Redeemer, freeing us from the chains of sin and redeeming us so that we could share in his divine life. May our prayer be: "I give you thanks, O God of my father; I praise you, O God my savior! I will make known your name, refuge of my life." (Sir 51:1)

93

2 Psalm 107:5-6 and 9   Only in the Lord

Hungry and thirsty, / their life was wasting away within them. / They cried to the Lord in their distress; / from their straits he rescued them. / Because he satisfied the longing soul / and filled the hungry soul with good things.

When we are oblivious of the Lord's abiding presence, or worse, stray away from him, we get lost in the wilderness of secular and temporal busyness which brings little or no joy and satisfaction. We find no fulfillment in the mundane and materialistic allurements which wean us away from the Lord.

With the psalmist let us thank the Lord, for he alone can satisfy our longing heart and fill our hungry soul with good things.

St. Peter points the way: "Lord, to whom shall we go? You have the words of eternal life." (Jn 6:68)

3 Psalm 107:10-11   Price of Sin

They dwelt in darkness and gloom, / bondsmen in want and in chains. / Because they had rebelled against the words of God / and scorned the counsel of the Most High.

Sin enslaves us. Its promise of happiness and good things to come soon fades and leaves us miserable, empty, and alone. We taste the bitter ashes of disillusionment.

The "words of God" and "the counsel of the Most High" may at times seem to be an unreasonably narrow road, but it is the only way to the peace and joy of the resurrection.

Jesus says to us also: "Your faith has been your salvation. Now go in peace." (Lk 7:50)

4 **Psalm 107:20 and 22   Healing Love**
He sent forth his word to heal them / and to snatch them from destruction. / Let them make thank offerings / and declare his works with shouts of joy.

The Father stated so unequivocally: "I, the Lord, am your healer" (Ex 15:26). Jesus began and continued his public ministry by healing all who came to him in faith. He wanted to be known as a healer. He healed not so much to display his divine power but to prove his tremendous compassion. The glory of Jesus today is to continue his healing mission among us. He asks only our faith.

When Jesus was asked if he could cure a possessed boy, he replied: "Everything is possible to a man who trusts." (Mk 9:23)

5 **Psalm 107:29-30   Peace Be Still**
He hushed the storm to a gentle breeze, / and the billows of the sea were stilled; / They rejoiced that they were calmed, / and he brought them to their desired haven.

Our life is often like a storm-tossed sea. When the waves of fear and anxiety, of trials and tribulations, of hardships and difficulties, seem insurmountable, we can call upon the Lord. He is always with us.

Jesus responds to our plight by hushing the winds and waves which disturb our peace and tranquillity. In the midst of our distress, Jesus approaches and says to us: "Get hold of yourselves! It is I. Do not be afraid!" (Mt 14:27)

6 **Psalm 107:35-37   The Harvest Is Rich**
He changed the desert into pools of water, / waterless land into water springs. / And there he settled the hungry, / and they built a city to dwell in. / They sowed fields and planted vineyards, / and they obtained a fruitful yield.

We look forward year after year to a bountiful harvest. We enjoy the fruit of the field, the yield of the vines, the nourishing vegetables of the garden.

All too seldom do we thank the Lord for the climatic conditions which produced the harvest, for the people who planted and nurtured the crops, for the people who transported and prepared it for us.

Jesus reminds us of the spiritual harvesting: "The harvest is rich but the workers are few; therefore ask the harvest-master to send workers to his harvest." (Lk 10:2)

7 **Psalm 107:42-43   Doers As Well**
The upright see this and rejoice, / and all wickedness closes its mouth. / Who is wise enough to observe these things / and to understand the favors of the Lord?

The Lord's caring love overshadows us, pouring down upon us all his gifts and blessings as we journey through life. The psalmist reminds us that only the upright and the wise recognize the goodness and the bounty of the Lord.

We must be upright not only to recognize his benevolence, but we also must be wise enough to use his gifts for his honor and glory and for our own salvation. Jesus warns us: "None of those who cry out, 'Lord, Lord,' will enter the kingdom of God but only the one who does the will of my Father in heaven." (Mt 7:21)

Temporal Refuge

A wildlife refuge is a sanctuary where birds and animals find protection and nourishment. Instinctively they seem to sense security and sustenance in these areas.

Our home is a hallowed refuge for us. It is a haven where we can relax and rest after the daily demands of duties, business, and work. There we find peace, but above all love.

When God is the head of our household, our refuge will be even more sacred and secure, peaceful and happy.

1 Psalm 5:12 Our Refuge Gives Joy

But let all who take refuge in you / be glad and exult forever. / Protect them, that you may be the joy / of those who love your name.

Daily we need to recall how much God loves us and how lovingly he watches over us. This psalm of morning prayer reminds us that God is always our refuge.

Through God's endless goodness and mercy, every new day brings fresh hope to us. This hope creates within us a positive attitude which helps us radiate the joy of the Lord along our path.

This truism is inherent in the angels' message: "You have nothing to fear! I come to proclaim good news to you—tidings of great joy to be shared by the whole people." (Lk 2:10)

2 Psalm 57:2-3 Plea for Protection

Have pity on me, O God; have pity on me, / for in you I take refuge. / In the shadow of your wings I take refuge, / till harm pass by. / I call to God the Most High, / to God my benefactor.

What a touching picture of God as our refuge, protecting us in the shadow of his wings "till harm pass by." Like the psalmist we must come to him with a humble, confident prayer and joyful trust. The Lord waits for our coming.

Please God, Jesus' lament will never include us: "How often have I wanted to gather your children together as a mother bird collects her young under her wings, and you refused me!" (Lk 13:34)

3 Psalm 59:17b-18 Count Your Blessings

You have been my stronghold, / my refuge in the day of distress. / O my strength! your praise will I sing; / for you, O God, are my stronghold, / my gracious God!

In times of distress and discouragement, in conflict and confusion, in trials and tribulation, we instinctively find a refuge in God, our gracious Father. How often we have experienced his comfort and consolation, his strength and peace!

With rejuvenated hope we want to sing his praises and we also pray: "Subject us not to the trial / but deliver us from the evil one." (Mt 6:13)

4 Psalm 64:11 Praise God Our Refuge
The just man is glad in the Lord and takes refuge in him; / in him glory all the upright of heart.

When we pause to recount the protective love with which the Lord envelops us, when we recall the numerous occasions when he came to our rescue when we were threatened or bombarded with problems and difficulties, then we can appreciate the refuge we have found in our loving Father.

This realization makes our hearts sing with joy, and we glory in the Lord's goodness to us.

St. Paul's prayer helps us glorify God: "May God, the source of all patience and encouragement, enable you to live in perfect harmony with one another according to the spirit of Christ Jesus, so that with one heart and voice you may glorify God, the Father of our Lord Jesus Christ." (Rom 15:5-6)

5 Psalm 91:11-12 Angels Guard You
For to his angels he has given command about you, / that they guard you in all your ways. / Upon their hands they shall bear you up, / lest you dash your foot against a stone.

As children we treasured the beautiful stories of our guardian angel sent by God to watch over us and protect us from harm. As we matured we might have lost some of the simplicity of that faith.

The psalmist reminds us once again of God's caring and concerned love as he sends his angels to "guard us in all our ways."

Today thank the Lord for his protective love! "See that you never despise one of these little ones. I assure you, their angels in heaven constantly behold my heavenly Father's face." (Mt 18:10)

6 Psalm 118:8-9
Trust Found Only in the Lord's Refuge

It is better to take refuge in the Lord / than to trust in man / It is better to take refuge in the Lord / than to trust in princes.

When difficulties arise, we usually seek advice from anyone who will listen to us. At times we may regret opening our heart to a certain person.

We are deeply disappointed when our trust is betrayed. It may happen that only after everything else fails we turn to the Lord and ask him to help us to decide and discern. Then we realize that we should have gone to him first.

St. Paul reminds us: "Praised be God, the Father of our Lord Jesus Christ, the Father of mercies, and the God of all consolation! He comforts us in all our afflictions and thus enables us to comfort those who are in trouble, with the same consolation we have received from him." (2 Cor 1:3-4)

7 Psalm 71:1-3   Refuge in Old Age

In you, O Lord, I take refuge; / let me never be put to shame. / In your justice rescue me, and deliver me; / incline your ear to me, and save me. / Be my rock of refuge, / a stronghold to give me safety, / for you are my rock and my fortress.

When age creeps up on us, we are prone to live in the past. At times we may be plagued with anxiety about past mistakes, neglect, or sinfulness. These are subtle attempts on the part of the evil one to discourage us about God's merciful forgiveness.

The Lord is a true refuge because he wants to forgive even more than we could desire it ourselves. Such compassion is a part of his divine love.

Our Blessed Mother herself assures us: "His mercy is from age to age / on those who fear him." (Lk 1:50)

Eternal Refuge

Our Father's house, or his presence, is a delightful refuge for us when we are weary and worn, distraught and discouraged. In the sanctuary of his presence we find comfort and consolation. There we can bask in his love which never fails us.

We will always find the welcome mat inviting us.

The Father invites us: "All you who are thirsty, / come to the water!" (Is 55:1)

Jesus invites us: "Come to me, all you who are weary. . . ." (Mt 11:28)

1 Psalm 16:1-2
No Refuge Apart from God

Keep me, O God, for in you I take refuge; / I say to the Lord, "My Lord are you. / Apart from you I have no good."

When we acknowledge our own human weakness, our inability, our inadequacy, then our prayer posture is similar to that of the psalmist when he admits: "Apart from you I have no good."

When we take refuge in the Lord and when we make him the first priority in our lives, then he will be our comfort and consolation in times of discouragement, doubt, fear, anxiety, bewilderment.

Jesus confirms this attitude: "Apart from me you can do nothing." (Jn 15:5)

2 Psalm 31:5-6 Safe in the Lord's Hands

You will free me from the snare they set for me, / for you are my refuge. / Into your hands I commend my spirit; / you will redeem me, O Lord, O faithful God.

Busyness and discouragement are two subtle snares which the evil one uses frequently to wean us away from the Lord. This brainwashing is so subtle that we are not even aware that it is taking place within us.

Jesus taught us by his attitude and example that the Lord must come first. Jesus was always concerned about doing the Father's will first and always.

This attitude was climaxed when he made the final gift of himself to the Father on the cross. "Father, into your hands I commend my spirit." (Lk 23:46)

3 Psalm 37:39-40 Salvation Our Final Refuge

The salvation of the just is from the Lord; / he is their refuge in time of distress. / And the Lord helps them and delivers them; / he delivers them from the wicked and saves them, / because they take refuge in him.

We may be perplexed at times at what appears to be a terrible injustice—the wicked seem to prosper while the good seem to suffer unjustly. Yet our faith tells us that God is just, rewarding the good and punishing the wicked.

If we are trying to live a good life, we may have to wait for some time, or even to the end of life, for our reward, but even this is a short time compared to the life awaiting us.

Then we will hear those welcome words of our Savior: "Come. You have my Father's blessing! Inherit the kingdom prepared for you from the creation of the world." (Mt 25:34)

4 Psalm 91:1-2   Acknowledge Your Refuge
You who dwell in the shelter of the Most High, / who abide in the shadow of the Almighty, / Say to the Lord, "My refuge and my fortress, / my God, in whom I trust."

In our baptism we have been incorporated into the body of Christ. As the adopted sons and daughters of the Father, we "dwell in the shelter and shadow of the Most High."

Our humble acknowledgement of the Lord as our refuge will make us more grateful. Thank him often for the privilege and protection of his love. Our gratitude will greatly increase our trust in him.

Jesus wants us to enjoy this privilege when he says: "Live on in my love." (Jn 15:9)

5 Psalm 91:9-10   Safe in Our Refuge
Because you have the Lord for your refuge; / you have made the Most High your stronghold. / No evil shall befall you, / nor shall affliction come near your tent.

When a young eagle is learning to fly, the mother bird hovers around her fledgling ready to swoop it up on her wings when it tires. The Old Testament writers use this same image in trying to describe God's protective care when dangers threaten us.

Given our weakened human nature, sin is always a menacing evil. With divine help we can avoid the pitfalls along the roadway of life.

Our faithful Father and refuge promises that help: "I bore you up on eagle wings and brought you here to myself." (Ex 19:4)

6 Psalm 119:113-114 Refuge of Hope
I hate men of divided heart, / but I love your law. / You are my refuge and my shield; / in your word I hope.

Jesus' word is trustworthy. His word outlines a way of life that will guarantee our eternal salvation. We will love his law when we discover that Jesus loves us so much that he wants us with him, and his law is the pathway leading us into that perfect union.

Jesus never tricked anyone into following him. He said it like it is—"take up your cross daily." His word instills hope in us. He asks us to trust him. Love begets trust. Surely he is our refuge.

Listen to his promise: "I solemnly assure you, / the man who hears my word / and has faith in him who sent me / possesses eternal life." (Jn 5:24)

7 Psalm 90:1-2 Refuge from All Eternity
O Lord, you have been our refuge / through all generations. / Before the mountains were begotten / and the earth and the world were brought forth, / from everlasting to everlasting you are God.

The eternity of God is graphically described by the psalmist as predating the creation of the earth and being before the mountains were begotten, not to mention his existing throughout all generations.

This reflection gives credibility to God's stability and fidelity and engenders great hope and confidence in us. His love for us is infinite and immutable. What further reassurance do we need?

St. Peter gives us some fatherly advice: "Grow rather in grace, and in the knowledge of our Lord and Savior Jesus Christ. Glory be to him now and to the day of eternity!" (2 Pt 3:18)

Safe Haven

M any of us are plagued with a sense of insecurity. We are timid and fearful. We need a secure haven to which we can flee when we are threatened. We need a friend who can give us reassurance, hope, and encouragement. We have such a friend in the Lord.

The Lord God is our haven in any storm. He is never far away but always at hand. The Father assures us: "Yes, when you seek me with all your heart, you will find me with you" (Jer 29:13f).

How grateful we are also to Jesus when he says: "And know that I am with you always, until the end of the world." (Mt 28:20)

1 Psalm 30:12-13   Endless Praise

You changed my mourning into dancing; / you took off my sackcloth and clothed me with gladness, / That my soul might sing praise to you without ceasing; / O Lord, my God, forever will I give you thanks.

Jesus prepared us for what we might expect in life as we follow him. There would be misunderstandings and persecution aplenty. At times the cross would seem intolerably cumbersome. We could expect heartaches and disappointments.

All these are only temporary. In the peace and joy which awaits us, our hearts will rejoice, our mourning will be turned into dancing, and we will sing God's praises.

St. Paul's words are comforting: "I consider the sufferings of the present to be as nothing compared with the glory to be revealed in us." (Rom 8:18)

2 Psalm 44:8-9 Squelching Satan

But you saved us from our foes, / and those who hated us you put to shame. / In God we gloried day by day; / your name we praised always.

Our principal foe is the evil one with all his subtle temptations and allurements. One of his clever schemes is to get us worried, anxious, and discouraged.

As the Holy Spirit enlightens us to recognize the temptations of the devil, we will be able to turn his inducements around to praise and glorify God. For such protective love, let us glorify God.

St. Paul gives us the key to discernment: ". . . nobody who speaks in the Spirit of God ever says, 'Cursed be Jesus.' And no one can say: 'Jesus is Lord,' except in the Holy Spirit." (1 Cor 12:3)

3 Psalm 50:14-15 Glorify the Lord

Offer to God praise as your sacrifice / and fulfill your vows to the Most High; / Then call upon me in time of distress; / I will rescue you, and you shall glorify me.

To sacrifice means to make holy. Our gifts offered to God become holy and sacred. When we offer praise, honor, and glory to God, it becomes a precious gift to our heavenly Father.

God cannot be outdone in generosity. When we call upon him in distress, he promises to rescue us so completely by his power and might that we are impelled to glorify him all our days.

St. Augustine says: "These are the sacrifices most pleasing to God: mercy, humility, praise, peace, charity."

Sirach reminds us: "The just man's sacrifice is most pleasing, / nor will it ever be forgotten. / In generous spirit pay homage to the Lord. . . ." (Sir 35:6f)

4 Psalm 54:8　Sacrifice of Praise

Freely will I offer you sacrifice; / I will praise your name, O Lord, for its goodness.

This psalm teaches us how to appeal humbly and confidently to God to protect and save us from any and all danger. Knowing God's faithfulness, we, like the psalmist, are certain that the Lord will always come to our rescue.

In return for his continual goodness to us, we promise God our praise and thanks as a very special gift. Pledging this gift to the Lord makes it a sacred sacrifice of praise.

The sacred writer urges us in these words: "Through him let us continually offer God a sacrifice of praise, that is, the fruit of lips which acknowledge his name." (Heb 13:15)

5 Psalm 107:32　Storm-tossed

Let them extol him in the assembly of the people / and praise him in the council of the elders.

The seafarers were storm-tossed and in great peril until the Lord hushed the storm to a gentle breeze and stilled the billows of the sea.

Our life is like the seafarers' voyage. We are threatened by the towering waves of difficulties and discouragement, by the mighty winds of worry and anxieties. When we cry to the Lord in our distress, we can be sure that he will rescue us. For his great goodness we want to praise the Lord not only privately, but we ought also to "extol him in the assembly of the people," that is, in our liturgical celebrations.

May the prayer of the Old Testament writer be our prayer also: "Save us, O God, our savior, / gather us and deliver us from the nations, / That we may give thanks to your holy name / and glory in praising you." (1 Chr 16:35)

6 **Psalm 108:6-7   His Loved Ones**
Be exalted above the heavens, O God; / over all the earth be your glory! / That your loved ones may escape, / help us by your right hand, and answer us.

In these few verses we have an ideal approach to prayer. In the first place, we praise God and beg that he "be exalted above the heavens and over all the earth." Thus we acknowledge his majesty and power.

Realizing that we can do nothing of ourselves, we beg him to come to our aid in times of trouble. We do so with confidence since we are his "loved ones." When we experience his saving help, as we are certain to do, we can sing our songs of praise and thanksgiving.

The apostle of love reminds us that we are loved: "See what love the Father has bestowed on us / in letting us be called children of God!" (1 Jn 3:1a)

7 **Psalm 109:1-2   Not of This World**
O God, whom I praise, be not silent, / for they have opened wicked and treacherous mouths against me.

The author prays for vindication from the calumnies leveled against him. He is suffering greatly because of their slander.

Jesus taught us that since he was persecuted we could expect to be persecuted also. He even advised us: "Be glad and rejoice, for your reward is great in heaven" (Mt 5:12). We rejoice by praising the Lord for permitting this opportunity to prepare us for heaven.

Jesus also explained why we would be persecuted: "If you find that the world hates you, / know it has hated me before you. / If you belonged to the world, / it would love you as its own; / the reason it hates you / is that you do not belong to the world." (Jn 15:18f)

Part VI
I Am the Way.
(Jn 14:6)

One Way—His Way

Every normal person wants to live a happy, healthy life filled with a good measure of peace and tranquillity.

If left to ourselves, we might mistakenly choose a road which would lead only to misery and unhappiness.

In the Psalms the Lord revealed the way to genuine happiness here and now and guarantee of happiness hereafter. We find some clear-cut directives which guide us along the right road.

Jesus augmented these directives when he proclaimed the Good News. The early Christians were accustomed to refer to the norms of Christian living as set down by Jesus simply as the Way. Let us prayerfully listen as the Holy Spirit outlines some of these directives as stated in the Psalms.

1 Psalm 86:11 His Way

Teach me, O Lord, your way / that I may walk in your truth; / direct my heart that it may fear your name.

The secret to a happy life filled with the Lord's peace and joy is simply to follow the way Jesus outlined for us. He is the Way. Keeping our heart's desire centered on him is the secret.

When our focus centers on Jesus, all the mundane concerns of life become rather peripheral. Jesus invites us to spend time with him, to pray with him, to listen to him in the depths of our being.

All this is included in his gracious invitation: "Come and see." (Jn 1:39)

2 Psalm 1:1-2 Highway to Happiness

Happy the man who follows not / the counsel of the wicked / Nor walks in the way of sinners, / nor sits in the company of the insolent, / But delights in the law of the Lord, / and meditates on his law day and night.

Notice the steps to our gradual downfall. We begin to "follow," then "walk" with, and finally to "sit in the company" of sinners. In brief, we toy with temptation, then we begin to rationalize and finally to convince ourselves that there is no wrong in what we wish to do.

On the contrary, "happy the man" who listens as Jesus says: "I am the way, and the truth, and the life." (Jn 14:6)

3 Psalm 1:3 By Their Fruits

He is like a tree / planted near running water, / That yields its fruit in due season, / and whose leaves never fade. / Whatever he does, prospers.

True happiness in life comes from listening to God's word and striving to fulfill his will perfectly in all our attitudes and activities. Our lives will reflect his goodness not only in major events but also in all the little happenings around us each day.

The fruit we bear is the reflection of his love, peace, and joy to all who cross our path.

Jesus says: "You can tell a tree by its fruit." (Mt 7:20)

4 Psalm 119:1-3   Walking with the Lord

Happy are they whose way is blameless, / who walk in the law of the Lord. / Happy are they who observe his decrees, / who seek him with all their heart, / And do no wrong, / but walk in his ways.

In his word, God reveals himself as a gracious Father pouring out his love upon us. In return he asks only our love.

Love always wants to please the beloved. The Lord gave us a way of life which is pleasing to him because it is the only way to real happiness for us here on earth and is a pledge of the eternal happiness in heaven.

Jesus tells us how to achieve this happiness: "Blest are they who hear the word of God and keep it." (Lk 11:28)

5 Psalm 101:2b-3a   Lifestyle

I will walk in the integrity of my heart, / within my house; / I will not set before my eyes / any base thing.

We are influenced by everything we see, hear, and experience in life. Some of these influences can be so subtle that we are not even aware of their pernicious influence on us. For example, haven't we often heard that something must be all right because "everybody is doing it"?

For this reason the psalmist urges us to walk in the integrity of our heart by keeping our ideal fixed on the Lord at all times. Then no "base thing" will overcome us. This is, and always will be, our daily struggle in life.

The Lord says to us as he did to St. Paul: "My grace is enough for you, for in weakness power reaches perfection." (2 Cor 12:9)

6 Psalm 139:1-3   Journey in Love

O Lord, you have probed me and you know me; / you know when I sit and when I stand; / you understand my thoughts from afar. / My journeys and my rest you scrutinize, / with all my ways you are familiar.

The Lord is omniscient and omnipresent. He sees and knows us no matter where we may be. He never leaves us, so much does he love us.

The Lord is not a passive observer on our journey through life. He abides with us to guide, protect, and assist us at every turn of the road.

Our walking in the Lord's way brings him much glory as Jesus informs us: "My Father has been glorified / in your bearing much fruit / and becoming my disciples." (Jn 15:8)

7 Psalm 101:1-2a   Single-hearted Service

Of kindness and judgment I will sing; / to you, O Lord, I will sing praise. / I will persevere in the way of integrity; / when will you come to me?

When we contemplate the goodness and the judgment of God, we discover how infinitely perfect the Lord is. Our hearts are overjoyed and our voices want to ring out his praise.

Our personal reaction to God's goodness should be a fervent desire to try to please him and serve him with integrity. This means doing his will with honesty, sincerity, and with undivided attention. Love must be our motivating power.

Jesus highlighted this attitude in the Beatitudes: "Blest are the single-hearted for they shall see God." (Mt 5:8)

Celebrate Life

Life is God's gracious gift to us. We want to live and enjoy every moment of our earthly existence. Even though hardships may arise, the expectation of a happier life spurs us on to accept in joy whatever may come.

We celebrate life as we breathe in God's fresh air, when we behold the beauty of his creation, when we are aware of his presence in the harmony of his handiwork, when we experience his love in the peace and joy which fills our hearts.

All of this is only a slight shadow of what is yet to come. Scripture tells us: "Eye has not seen, ear has not heard, / nor has it so much as dawned on man / what God has prepared for those who love him." (1 Cor 2:9)

1 Psalm 119:50   Divine Comforter
My comfort in my affliction is / that your promise gives me life.

There is great mystery involved in suffering and affliction. The mystery is too deep for our limited intellects to fathom.

Yet we know that there is not a single pain suffered in vain. Jesus suffered every affliction which could ever come our way; thus he sanctified suffering. Suffering has thus become our stepping-stone into a more intimate union with him.

St. Paul's words are consoling: "He comforts us in all our affliction and thus enables us to comfort those who are in trouble, with the same consolation we have received from him." (2 Cor 1:4)

2 Psalm 119:93 Jesus Is the Way
Never will I forget your precepts, / for through them you give me life.

Jesus came into the world not only to teach us the precepts which would lead us to eternal life, but he lived the pattern of life which he wants us to follow. We become his disciples when we not only follow him but when we live the lifestyle that he showed us by his own example.

He could rightly say: "... learn from me, for I am gentle and humble of heart" (Mt 11:29).

He could also say to us: "What I just did was to give you an example: / as I have done, so you must do." (Jn 13:15)

3 Psalm 119:107 Healing Presence
I am very much afflicted; / O Lord, give me life according to your word.

Life is a litany of ups and downs, of hills and valleys, of joys and sorrows. In the midst of life's happenings, we must continually remind ourselves we are not walking alone. The Lord is with us every step of the way.

He is within us, among us, and beyond us. He promised us that he would never leave us but would be with us until the end of the world.

Jesus promised us the fullness of life when he said: "I came that they might have life / and have it to the full." (Jn 10:10)

4 Psalm 119:109   Paradox
Though constantly I take my life in my hands, / yet I forget not your law.

Persecution has always been rampant in the church. In some areas a person may say, "I take my life in my hands," when he tries to live his Christian way of life. More often the persecution is more subtle. It may come in the form of discrimination. It may be a constant bombardment of sly remarks, ridicule, and insults.

We find great encouragement in the promise of Jesus: "Blest are you when they insult you and persecute you / and utter every kind of slander against you because of me. / Be glad and rejoice, for your reward is great in heaven." (Mt 5:11-12a)

5 Psalm 119:149   No Greater Kindness
Hear my voice according to your kindness, O Lord; / according to your ordinance give me life.

God is a solicitous Father, eager and anxious to help us. He endowed us with a free will and he greatly respects our freedom. For this reason he waits for us to ask for his help. He will not force himself upon us.

Jesus assures us that whatever we ask in his name, the Father will give us. Asking in Jesus' name means living according to the ordinance God has given us.

Jesus encourages us when he says: "I give you my assurance, / whatever you ask the Father, / he will give you in my name." (Jn 16:23)

6 Psalm 119:154   Redeeming Love
Plead my cause, and redeem me; / for the sake of your promise give me life.

When Jesus died on the cross, he did not simply pay the penalty of our sins, but he redeemed our fallen human nature. He gave us the capacity to receive his divine life. This is just a foretaste of the fullness of that life we will enjoy with him in heaven.

Only after we shed this mortal body will we be able to share in that union of perfect love which is his divine life.

St. Paul explains this union: "Through baptism into his death we were buried with him, so that, just as Christ was raised from the dead by the glory of the Father, we too might live a new life." (Rom 6:4)

7 Psalm 119:159   Yes, Lord
See how I love your precepts, O Lord; / in your kindness give me life.

In the biblical sense of the term, "precepts" are not so much commandments, rules, and regulations as we understand them. Rather they are revelations and directives showing us how we ought to live in order to respond to the love God is pouring out upon us.

Precepts are a way and means of giving ourselves and all that we do and are as a special love offering to the Lord. This pleases him very much. This expression of love causes us to grow and develop a deep, personal relationship with our gracious Father. Jesus teaches us how to love: "You will live in my love / if you keep my commandments, / even as I have kept my Father's commandments." (Jn 15:10)

Look Redeemed

Throughout the Psalter, we hear prayers ranging between two extremes. We hear desperate cries begging God for his mercy and his saving power, and then shouts of joy and exultation thanking God for his great gift of salvation.

These expressions give us compelling reasons for gratitude and rejoicing. Jesus came as our Savior and Redeemer. We know he will save us if we permit him. Frequently we hear Jesus saying to us in his word as he did to the sinful woman: "Your faith has been your salvation" (Lk 7:50).

As we pray with his word this week, may all our actions and attitudes radiate this overwhelming truth. "Look to him that you may be radiant with joy." (Ps 34:6)

1 Psalm 67:2-3 Only Ask

May God have pity on us and bless us; / may he let his face shine upon us. / So may your way be known upon earth; / among all nations, your salvation.

Our prayer of petition is always pleasing to God. It manifests our dependence upon him. It assures our faithful Father that we love him and trust him.

The more frequently we repeat our petition, the more it is enforced and clarified in our own minds. As we beg God repeatedly to save us, we are automatically directing our path in the way he made known to us. We never journey alone; we are also attracting others to our way of life.

Jesus prophesied that he would draw all men: "I—once I am lifted up from the earth— / will draw all men to myself." (Jn 12:32)

2 Psalm 85:3-4 A Forgiving God

You have forgiven the guilt of your people; / you have covered all their sins. / You have withdrawn all your wrath; / you have revoked your burning anger.

When we speak of God as being angry, grieved, or outraged, we are speaking anthropomorphically. We have no other way of expressing the divine realities beyond us.

St. Thomas says: "God is not offended by us except insofar as we act against our own proper good."

The Father speaking through the prophet Hosea says: "My heart is overwhelmed, / my pity is stirred. / I will not give vent to my blazing anger... / For I am God and not man, / the Holy One present among you; / I will not let the flames consume you." (Hos 11:8c-9)

3 Psalm 98:2 and 3b
Symbol Sacred and Sublime

The Lord has made his salvation known: / in the sight of the nations he has revealed his justice. / All the ends of the earth have seen / the salvation by our God.

In the Old Testament times, God's promise of a redeemer was kept alive by the prayers and predictions of the prophets. The Lord did not want his people to lose hope but to continue to plead and prepare for the coming of the Redeemer.

In our day the cross and the crucifix prominently displayed on our buildings, in our homes, on our person, keep before us the saving, redeeming love which God holds out to us.

How thrilling are the words of St. John: "Yes, God so loved the world / that he gave his only Son, / that whoever believes in him may not die / but may have eternal life." (Jn 3:16)

4 Psalm 119:123 *Ecce Homo*
My eyes strain after your salvation / and your just promise.

When Pilate presented the pitiable sight of Jesus scourged and crowned with thorns before the crowd, he cried: "Behold the Man!" (*"Ecce Homo!"*) Pilate did not know that he was offering redemption and salvation not only to the crowd before him but to the whole world.

The psalmist says that his "eyes strain after salvation" as he awaits the "just promise" of the Lord. We no longer have to wait. We have the Redeemer living with us and within us. What is more, he is aiding and assisting us on our way toward our eternal salvation. What a privileged people we are! Pilate said: "Look at the man!" (Jn 19:5)

5 Psalm 40:11 Proclaim the Good News
Your justice I kept not hid within my heart; / your faithfulness and your salvation I have spoken of; / I have made no secret of your kindness and your truth / in the vast assembly.

God needs us. He has called us. He has endowed us with the gift of faith. He has made known to us the good news of our redemption and salvation.

Our trusting Father has commissioned us to proclaim the good news of salvation to the whole world. Our attitudes, our actions, our words are all channels by which we disseminate God's faithfulness in granting us eternal salvation.

Jesus sent us forth with these words: "Go into the whole world and proclaim the good news to all creation." (Mk 16:15)

6 Psalm 50:23   Paving the Way
"He that offers praise as a sacrifice glorifies me; / and to him that goes the right way I will / show the salvation of God."

To sacrifice means to make something holy. A gift freely and lovingly given becomes holy when offered to God. The gift of ourselves with hearts filled with praise and thanksgiving is indeed precious to our gracious Father.

As we rejoice in the privilege of offering him a sacrifice of praise, we are paving the way to our own eternal salvation. We are also encouraging others to join our entourage joyously.

St. Paul said it so well: "Everyone should see how unselfish you are." (Phil 4:5)

7 Psalm 40:17   The Lord Be Glorified
But may all who seek you / exult and be glad in you, / And may those who love your salvation / say ever, "The Lord be glorified."

There cannot be any greater gift than our eternal salvation. As we strive to achieve this goal in life, we find great delight and joy in the expectation of the indescribable happiness which awaits us.

Our soul is filled to overflowing. Our heart longs to burst forth with praise, glory, and thanks to so gracious a Father.

The prophet helps us to proclaim the glory of God: "I rejoice heartily in the Lord, / in my God is the joy of my soul; / For he has clothed me with a robe of salvation, / and wrapped me in a mantle of justice. . . ." (Is 61:10)

Charted Course

Jesus taught us a way of life which will bring joy and happiness into our earthly sojourn. He did even more. He not only mapped out the way for us but also led that way of life himself. He is our prime model and example on our journey heavenward.

We have been blessed with the gift of faith and supplied with all our needs along the charted course. As we recall all our blessings, joy and gratitude wells up within us. Our gratitude naturally breaks out in praise, honor, and glory to so good a God.

This week beg all the hosts of heaven, especially our departed loved ones, to join us in praising and glorifying the Father, Son, and Holy Spirit.

1 Psalm 19:5 Praise Worldwide

Through all the earth their voice resounds, / and to the ends of the world, their message.

We, too, are invited to let our voices resound with the praise of the Lord. Our special mission in life is to become channels through which the peace and joy of the Lord may flow out to others.

If we ourselves are at peace, then there is at least some peace in the world. If we share our peace with everyone we meet, then everyone will be at peace. Then all our voices will resound with the praise and glory of God.

Let us pray with St. Paul: "Praised be the God and Father of our Lord Jesus Christ, who has bestowed on us in Christ every spiritual blessing in the heavens!" (Eph 1:3)

2 Psalm 29:1-2 Clothed in Majesty

Give to the Lord, you sons of God, / give to the Lord glory and praise, / Give to the Lord the glory due his name; / adore the Lord in holy attire.

Truly we are the daughters and sons of God. Our Father adopted us as his children at the moment of our baptism. We enjoy a unique dignity—an extraordinary privilege, an extra-terrestrial and eternal relationship.

For all of this we give God all the glory and praise. We praise him especially for his "holy attire" which is all the attributes from which we receive so many blessings.

Jesus tells us how important we are to the Father: "My Father has been glorified / in your bearing much fruit / and becoming my disciples." (Jn 15:8)

3 Psalm 48:2-3 Divine Dwelling Place

Great is the Lord and wholly to be praised / in the city of our God. / His holy mountain, fairest of heights, / is the joy of all the earth.

For the Israelite, the temple was sacred because God dwelt there. Jerusalem was "the city of God." Mount Zion was "his holy mountain." God's presence was the reason for his joy. It called forth his praise.

By virtue of our baptism we, Christians, are the temple of God, the city of God, and his holy mountain. With joyful hearts, we too can sing lustily and loudly: "Great is the Lord and wholly to be praised."

St. Paul assures us that we are temples of the Holy Spirit: "Are you not aware that you are the temple of God, and that the Spirit of God dwells in you? If anyone destroys God's temple, God will destroy him." (1 Cor 3:16-17)

4 Psalm 69:31-32   True Worship
I will praise the name of God in song, / and I will glorify him with thanksgiving; / This will please the Lord more than oxen / or bullocks with horns and divided hooves.

The writer recognizes that proper dispositions of mind and heart are essential to divine worship. Mere lip service or ritualistic offerings are empty and not pleasing to God.

Likewise our praise and thanksgiving must be sincere, coming from the depth of our being. Jesus cautioned us about authentic worship in spirit and truth. He lamented: "This people pays me lip service / but their heart is far from me." (Mt 15:8; cf. Is 29:13)

5 Psalm 119:164   Pray without Ceasing
Seven times a day I praise you / for your just ordinances.

Seven is a sacred number for the Hebrews. It symbolizes perfection. For us it suggests that we should turn our thoughts to the Lord in praise many times throughout the course of the day. We should praise him always and everywhere.

The apostle Paul urges us to pray always, to pray without ceasing. We can do so when we praise the Lord for his ordinances which guide us along the road to happiness in this life and eternal joy in the hereafter.

When Peter asked Jesus if it was sufficient to forgive seven times, Jesus was quick to respond: "Not seven times, but seventy times seven times." Then Jesus added: "My heavenly Father will treat you in exactly the same way unless each of you forgives his brother from his heart." (Mt 18:35)

6 **Psalm 119:171-172 Pathways to Praise**
My lips pour forth your praise, / because you teach me your statutes. / May my tongue sing of your promise, / for all your commands are just.

We find eight synonyms in this lengthy psalm to describe God's statutes, promises, commands. They have a single purpose and that is to point out the solicitous care of the Father that we should have sufficient directives to guide us through the maze of daily living in this land of exile.

For this gracious care, should not our "lips pour forth his praise?" Over and above these many directives, Jesus' lifestyle is our model and example: "I am the way, and the truth, and the life" (Jn 14:6). "What I just did was to give you an example: / as I have done, so you must do." (Jn 13:15)

7 **Psalm 140:14 Praise Prevails**
Surely the just shall give thanks to your name; / the upright shall dwell in your presence.

If we want to be numbered among the just, and who of us doesn't, if we are striving for a personal relationship with our Father, then the psalmist expects us to praise and thank the Lord.

The most effective way we can offer praise to God is by our lifestyle. As we seriously try to follow the way of life which Jesus set forth, as we try to walk in his footsteps, then we are praising and thanking God.

Did not Jesus himself say: "My Father has been glorified / in your bearing much fruit / and becoming my disciples." (Jn 15:8)

PART VII

Taking Bread and Giving Thanks

(Lk 22:19)

We Thank You, Father

E very normal human being has an inherent sense of gratitude. If we are grateful to others for all they do for us, how much greater should be our gratitude to God.

Our prayer of thanksgiving helps us to recognize the goodness in other people. It leads us to appreciate the goodness in all of creation, and above all it makes us more aware of the goodness of God our Creator and Redeemer.

May every day be a thanksgiving day!

1 Psalm 105:1-2   Wondrous Deeds

Give thanks to the Lord, invoke his name; / make known among the nations his deeds. / Sing to him, sing his praise, / proclaim all his wondrous deeds.

This psalm recalls the wondrous deeds the Lord has done in freeing the chosen people from the slavery of Egypt. Similarly, by his passion, death, and resurrection Jesus freed us from the bondage of sin.

Today, pause frequently to whisper a brief thank you to the Lord for the gift of salvation.

Jesus himself told us: "The Father loves me for this: / That I lay down my life / to take it up again." (Jn 10:17)

2 **Psalm 126:5-6   Joyful Hope**
Those that sow in tears shall reap rejoicing. / Although they go forth weeping, /carrying the seed to be sown, / They shall come back rejoicing, / carrying their sheaves.

Our pathway through life is often beset with problems, worries, and anxieties. We see our plans thwarted, our projects fail, our best intentions misunderstood.

At times what seems to be a tragic and traumatic experience turns out with time to be a blessing.

Jesus is our exemplar: "As we have shared much in the suffering of Christ, so through Christ do we share abundantly in his consolation." (2 Cor 1:5)

3 **Psalm 116:17   Sacrifice of Thanksgiving**
To you will I offer sacrifice of thanksgiving, / and I will call upon the name of the Lord.

In the Mass we have a unique privilege of offering our "sacrifice of thanksgiving" to the Father. The Father asks only one gift from us and that is the gift of ourselves. As we unite all our prayers, works, and sufferings in union with Jesus, our eternal high priest, we are making our sacrifice of thanksgiving.

Jesus unites our gift with his own gift, thus adding an infinite dimension to our gift. "Through him let us continually offer God a sacrifice of praise, that is, the fruit of lips which acknowledge his name." (Heb 13:15)

4 Psalm 100:4-5 Bless His Name
Enter his gates with thanksgiving, / his courts with praise; / Give thanks to him; bless his name, for he is good: / the Lord, whose kindness endures forever, / and his faithfulness, to all generations.

Gratitude is deeply ingrained in our human nature. As we prayerfully pause to reflect on the Lord's enduring kindness in energizing, sustaining, and providing for us, our hearts swell with the joy of love and gratitude.

Daily we need to pause to express our gratitude. We need to manifest our appreciation by using well the Lord's gifts to us.

St. Paul reminds us of God's favor upon us: "He likewise predestined us through Christ Jesus to be his adopted sons—such was his will and pleasure—that all might praise the glorious favor he has bestowed on us in his beloved." (Eph 1:5-6)

5 Psalm 118:28-29 Give Thanks
You are my God, and I give thanks to you; / O my God, I extol you. / Give thanks to the Lord, for he is good; / for his kindness endures forever.

Our prayer of thanksgiving to the Lord is a high form of prayer, next to the prayer of praise. The more grateful we are, the more prayerful will we become.

To whom do we owe more gratitude than to the Lord himself who gave us everything—not only the gifts in the temporal order for our life on earth but also the multiplicity of all his spiritual gifts, including the gift of himself.

Visit with the Lord today and thank him for each individual gift as it comes to mind.

With Jesus let us say often: "Father, I thank you for having heard me." (Jn 11:41)

6 Psalm 106:1-2 Enduring Kindness

Give thanks to the Lord, for he is good, / for his kindness endures forever. / Who can tell the mighty deeds of the Lord, / or proclaim all his praises?

As we pause to reflect on God's unlimited and unceasing providential love for our wayward world, our hearts are filled with admiration and gratitude.

Recalling his caring and concerned love for us throughout all the days of our own life, our hearts want to burst forth with praise and thanksgiving. Surely "his kindness endures forever."

With fatherly concern St. Paul advises us: "Give thanks to God the Father always and for everything in the name of our Lord Jesus Christ." (Eph 5:20)

7 Psalm 86:12 God of All Goodness

I will give thanks to you, O Lord my God, / with all my heart, / and I will glorify your name forever.

Our Father is a most gracious God. He is the source of all good. He lavishes his gifts most generously upon us. Like the pause that refreshes we need to pause from time to time to express our prayerful thanks.

A prayerful person will also be a grateful person. When we spend time in prayer, we bring ourselves to a greater awareness of God's kindness to us. With all our heart we want to glorify so good a father.

St. Paul's admonition is brief and to the point: "Dedicate yourselves to thankfulness." (Col 3:15)

Liturgical Thanksgiving

We will never be able to repay our personal debt of gratitude to God. However, our Father is greatly pleased with our every attempt to thank him.

God is even more pleased when we gather as his people to express our gratitude in celebration. Jesus taught us the importance of liturgical prayer: "He came to Nazareth ... entering the synagogue on the sabbath as he was in the habit of doing ..." (Lk 4:16).

Jesus did even more. He gave us the Mass in which he accepts our personal thanksgiving along with the thanksgiving of all our assembled brothers and sisters, and he unites it to the gift of himself and presents it to the Father in our name. This is the only way we can render fitting thanks to our provident Father.

1 Psalm 35:18   Greater Glory

I will give you thanks in the vast assembly, / in the mighty throng I will praise you.

We are social beings. We need one another. As we assemble we are encouraged and supported by one another's presence. Our own thanks and gratitude to God is enhanced as together we raise our hearts and voices in praising and thanking God.

St. Paul's words express it so well: "Indeed, everything is ordered to your benefit, so that the grace bestowed in abundance may bring greater glory to God because they who give thanks are many." (2 Cor 4:15)

2 Psalm 42:5   Journeying in Joy
Those times I recall, / now that I pour out my soul within me, / When I went with the throng / and led them in procession to the house of God, / Amid loud cries of joy and thanksgiving.

When we join "in procession to the house of God" and when we unite our voices in "loud cries of joy and thanksgiving," our spirit is recharged, our enthusiasm rekindled, our zest renewed to face the routine tasks of each day.

There is great wisdom in the church's law encouraging us to pause, rest, and relax weekly to worship and thank our gracious Father for his inestimable blessings.

In his pastoral zeal St. Paul said it succinctly: "Rejoice always, never cease praying, render constant thanks; such is God's will for you in Christ Jesus." (1 Thes 5:16-18)

3 Psalm 43:4   Table of the Lord
Then I will go in to the altar of God, / the God of my gladness and joy; / Then will I give thanks upon the harp, / O God, my God!

The liturgy of the church is directed toward offering praise and thanksgiving to the Father. As we join in singing the psalms, hymns, and the various parts of the Eucharistic Celebration, we are giving thanks to God "with gladness and joy."

Furthermore, as we unite with our brothers and sisters in Christ, our corporate prayer of thanksgiving becomes even more pleasing to our loving Father.

St. Paul reminds us of our identity as a worshipping family: "Because the loaf of bread is one, we, many though we are, are one body, for we all partake of the one loaf." (1 Cor 10:17)

4 Psalm 108:4   Called to Thankfulness
I will give thanks to you among the peoples, O Lord; / I will chant your praise among the nations.

We are "a chosen race, a royal priesthood, a holy nation, a people he claims for his own to proclaim the glorious works of the One who called you from darkness into his marvelous light" (1 Pt 2:9).

It behooves us to assemble to offer our thanksgiving to God for his gifts upon us and upon all others. It is our duty to thank God for others, and our mission is to follow the example of our loving Father who lets his sun rise on the bad and good, and his rain fall on the just and unjust. For all his blessings let us thank him.

What a privilege is ours: "Thanks be to God for his indescribable gift!" (2 Cor 9:15)

5 Psalm 111:1-2   His Wondrous Works
I will give thanks to the Lord with all my heart / in the company and assembly of the just. / Great are the works of the Lord, / exquisite in all their delights.

When we gather for some liturgical celebration, our own faith is strengthened by the presence of many others assembled to praise and thank God with us.

This releases the well-springs of joy and gratitude in our own hearts. Our appreciation and thanksgiving is enriched and deepened as we verbalize these sentiments welling up in our hearts.

This happened to the disciples on one occasion: "... the entire crowd of disciples began to rejoice and praise God loudly for the display of power they had seen. ..." (Lk 19:37)

6 Psalm 116:17
Eucharist Means Thanksgiving

To you will I offer sacrifice of thanksgiving, / and I will call upon the name of the Lord.

When Jesus instituted the Eucharist, he gave us a perfect way to offer our thanks to the Father. The Mass is an oblation. Eucharist means thanksgiving; hence it is an ideal method of offering thanks to the Lord.

Jesus invites us to offer the gift of ourselves in thanksgiving. Jesus unites our gift with the gift of himself, thus giving our thanks an infinite dimension.

At the Last Supper, Jesus showed us the way: "Then, taking bread and giving thanks, he broke it and gave it to them, saying: 'This is my body to be given for you.'" (Lk 22:19)

7 Psalm 138:2   You Are That Temple

I will worship at your holy temple / and give thanks to your name, / Because of your kindness and your truth; / for you have made great above all things / your name and your promise.

God has created for himself a unique temple within us. In redeeming our sinful human nature, Jesus made us the temple of the Holy Spirit. Who can fathom so overwhelming a love? The mere thought fills our hearts to overflowing with gratitude.

St. Paul reminds us that we need to recall this truth often: "You must know that your body is a temple of the Holy Spirit, who is within—the Spirit you have received from God. You are not your own. You have been purchased, and at a price! So glorify God in your body." (1 Cor 6:19-20)

Eucharist—Thanksgiving

E ven though the chosen people of the Old
Testament had no notion of the Eucharist,
sacred meals were very much a part of their rituals.
They believed that God communicated something
of himself to them as they partook of these meals.

In the psalms we discover some signs and
symbols prefiguring the presence of the Lord in
the Eucharist. God was carefully and methodically
preparing us for his heavenly gift.

As we pray the suggested passages for this week,
we will come to a greater appreciation of the
precious gift which is ours in the Eucharist.

For this tremendous treasure, let us give thanks.

1 Psalm 78:23b-24   What Is This?
*The doors of heaven he opened; / He rained manna
upon them for food / and gave them heavenly bread.*

When the Israelites first saw the manna on the
desert floor, they were mystified and asked,
"Manna?" which means "What is this?" Moses
told them: "This is the bread which the Lord has
given you to eat" (Ex 16:15).

As we ponder the mystery of the Eucharist, we
too are overwhelmed by the goodness of God.
Every day he opens the doors of heaven to give us
heavenly bread, to nourish and strengthen us, to
encourage and guide us, to comfort and console
us.

Jesus promised us: "This is the bread that came
down from heaven. / Unlike your ancestors who
ate and died nonetheless, / the man who feeds on
this bread shall live forever." (Jn 6:58)

137

2 Psalm 105:40 Thorough Preparation
They asked, and he brought them quail, / and with bread from heaven he satisfied them.

God painstakingly prepared the people for this great mystery of the Eucharist. The water from the rock on Mt. Horeb and the manna in the desert prefigured the true gift of bread from heaven.

When the appointed time came, Jesus also prepared us for this incomprehensible gift. He meticulously prepared us by changing water into wine, by multiplying bread to feed the multitude. He discoursed at great length about the gift of himself as the bread of heaven.

Ponder his precious words: "This is my body to be given for you. . . . This cup is the new covenant in my blood, which will be shed for you." (Lk 22:19-20)

3 Psalm 104:14b-15 Bread and Wine
Producing bread from the earth / and wine to gladden men's hearts.

For the Semite, bread and wine were the symbols of God's providential care. Bread and wine signified the graciousness and goodness of God in supplying all their needs as they journeyed through life.

It seems only natural that Jesus chose bread and wine to signify his presence in the Eucharist. Jesus abides with us eucharistically to assure us that he will always supply all our spiritual needs during our earthly sojourn.

Jesus promised: "No one who comes to me shall ever be hungry, / no one who believes in me shall ever thirst." (Jn 6:35)

4 Psalm 78:25   Bread of Angels
The bread of the mighty was eaten by men; / even a surfeit of provisions he sent them.

In Scripture, the angels are often called "the mighty." Not only did the Lord give us the bread of angels but he also continues to give us an overabundance of his gifts.

In many ancient rituals the worshipper always ate some of the gift offered in sacrifice. Meals serve to express the communication of divine life which God gives to his people.

How completely and totally Jesus communicates his divine life to us in the Eucharist! All this he implied in these few words: "I myself am the living bread / come down from heaven. / If anyone eats this bread / he shall live forever." (Jn 6:51)

5 Psalm 116:12-13   Cup of Salvation
How shall I make a return to the Lord / for all the good he has done for me? / The cup of salvation I will take up, / and I will call upon the name of the Lord.

At one time in the Mass, these words were part of the priest's private prayer before receiving the Precious Blood. They contain much inspiration for our reflection.

We are reminded by these words that we can never repay such goodness on the part of Jesus in giving us himself in the Eucharist. However, one of the best ways to express our appreciation and gratitude is to use well the gifts the Lord has given us. Our receiving Holy Communion brings much joy to the heart of Jesus.

Listen to his own words: "This cup is the new covenant in my blood, which will be shed for you." (Lk 22:20)

6 Psalm 41:10 To Whom Shall We Go?
Even my friend who had my trust / and partook of my bread, has raised his heel against me.

The perfidy of Judas caused Jesus great pain. He was present at the Last Supper and then proceeded to carry out his plan to betray Jesus to his enemies.

Unfortunately, even today Jesus sees many of his friends deserting him even though he has personally invited them to partake of his eucharistic banquet.

The next time you receive Holy Communion, add an extra note of fervor and gratitude for this tremendous gift.

May we never hear Jesus say to us: "Do you want to leave me too?" (Jn 6:67)

7 Psalm 52:11 Thank You, Lord
I will thank you always for what you have done, / and proclaim the goodness of your name / before your faithful ones.

Each time we offer the Eucharist with our brothers and sisters in Christ, we are praising and glorifying God for his wonders. We are also thanking him for all the good which accrues to us from the Eucharist.

Eucharist means gratitude. In turn, gratitude is the source of thanksgiving. In order to be truly grateful, we need to remember. Thanksgiving is always accompanied by remembrance.

This is precisely why Jesus said: "Do this as a remembrance of me." (Lk 22:19)

Unspeakable Gift

In the upper room the night before he died, Jesus gave us the gift of himself in the Eucharist—a gift beyond our human comprehension. He loves us so much, he could not leave us orphans. He even accommodated himself to our humanness by giving us a sign and symbol of his eucharistic presence—bread and wine.

Jesus was so overjoyed in giving us the gift of himself that he climaxed the ceremony by singing hymns of praise and thanksgiving. "Then after singing songs of praise, they walked out to the Mount of Olives" (Mt 26:30).

When we try to fathom the mystery of Jesus' tremendous love for us, our hearts, too, ring out with songs of praise and thanksgiving.

1 Psalm 30:2-3   Thanksgiving for Healing
I will extol you, O Lord, for you drew me clear / and did not let my enemies rejoice over me. / O Lord, my God, / I cried out to you and you healed me.

Thus the psalmist thanks God for having restored him to health. We can so easily take our own good health for granted. How many times the Lord has healed us from illnesses such as colds, minor injuries, or even more serious maladies.

Today let us take the occasion to thank the Lord for the gift of life and also for our own health.

Listen to St. Paul's advice: "Rejoice always, never cease praying, render constant thanks; such is God's will for you in Christ Jesus" (1 Thes 5:16-18). Jesus says to us also: "Be on your way. Your faith has healed you." (Mk 10:52)

2 Psalm 35:28 Joyful Remembering

Then my tongue shall recount your justice, / your praise, all the day.

We cannot have a genuine celebration without a memorial. As we recall some of the great blessings we have received, our hearts are filled with joy and gratitude.

As we pause to recount the Lord's unparalleled goodness and blessings upon us, our hearts will be lifted up in "praise all the day." Today, pause to recount some of the blessings of this past week. Then you will rejoice.

Our greatest blessing is the Eucharist. "This is my body, which is for you. Do this in remembrance of me." (1 Cor 11:24)

3 Psalm 45:18 Always and Everywhere

I will make your name memorable / through all generations; / therefore shall nations praise you / forever and ever.

How can we make the Lord's name "memorable through all generations"? Is this wishful thinking or idle fantasy? By no means!

When we praise and thank God for himself and all his beneficence, we are influencing others to do the same. They, in turn, normally will pass on this spirit of grateful praise to their children and on through succeeding generations. Recalling the worldwide influence of St. Therese of Lisieux or St. Francis, we can be certain that all nations will praise the Lord.

Jesus encourages us in our mission of making him known: "Whoever acknowledges me before men I will acknowledge before my Father in heaven." (Mt 10:32)

4 Psalm 63:6   Rich Banquet

As with the riches of a banquet shall my / soul be satisifed, / and with exultant lips my mouth shall praise you.

A banquet is a time of celebration, of delightful company, of fine food, of delicate wine.

In Scripture much more is meant by a banquet. A banquet, or even an ordinary meal, means an intimate personal relationship with the Lord. God communicates himself and his divine life through the partaking of food. This is why Jesus gave himself as food in the eucharistic banquet.

Jesus is speaking of this intimacy when he says: "Here I stand, knocking at the door. If anyone hears me calling and opens the door, I will enter his house and have supper with him, and he with me." (Rev. 3:20)

5 Psalm 113:1-2   No Greater Name

Praise, you servants of the Lord, / praise the name of the Lord. / Blessed be the name of the Lord / both now and forever.

Here is fervent prayer for God to be acknowledged, adored, and glorified at all times and in all places. As we make these words our prayer, we find ourselves thanking and praising God more earnestly. God is worthy of our praise because of his boundless goodness to us, his servants. In begging that the name of the Lord may be praised "both now and forever," we ourselves are being transformed.

St. Paul prays for our progress: "We pray for you always that our God may make you worthy of his call. . . . In this way the name of our Lord Jesus may be glorified in you and you in him, in accord with the gracious gift of our God and of the Lord Jesus Christ." (2 Thes 1:11-12)

6 Psalm 113:3 From East to West
From the rising to the setting of the sun / is the name of the Lord to be praised.

This poetic expression includes two important dimensions. We are praying that the name of the Lord may be praised all day long from morning until evening. It also means that we ask that people everywhere from east to the west be formed into a people of praise. To be more prosaic, we pray that God be praised everywhere and always, beginning with ourselves.

How wonderfully are the words of the prophet fulfilled today: "For from the rising of the sun, even to its setting, / my name is great among the nations; / And everywhere they bring sacrifice to my name, / and a pure offering; . . ." (Mal 1:11)

7 Psalm 117:1-2 Fragrant Aroma
Praise the Lord, all you nations; / glorify him, all you peoples! / For steadfast is his kindness toward us, / and the fidelity of the Lord endures forever.

This is the shortest psalm in the Psalter, but it embraces all nations and penetrates the universal kingdom which Jesus founded. It is a brief hymn of praise calling all peoples to praise and glorify God especially for his fidelity in keeping all his promises.

Our fervent prayer should be that the Lord would be accepted, revered, and loved by all nations. If this would take place, we would be living in the vestibule of heaven.

Listen to St. Paul's words: "Thanks be to God, who unfailingly leads us on in Christ's triumphal train, and employs us to diffuse the fragrance of his knowledge everywhere! We are an aroma of Christ for God's sake. . . ." (2 Cor 2:14-15a)

Part VIII

All You Ask the Father in My Name

(Jn 15:16)

Prayer of Petition

The prayer of petition is not only a constant one in our devotional life but also a very important one. Asking for God's help bears much fruit in our spiritual growth.

It reminds us of our total dependence upon our loving Father.

Our repeated requests purify our desire from the dross of self-seeking and selfishness.

Renewing our prayer of petition makes our desire more ardent.

Persevering in our prayer will enable us to use well the gifts the Lord bestows on us.

1 Psalm 4:2   A God Who Listens

When I call, answer me, O my just God, / you who relieve me when I am in distress; / have pity on me, and hear my prayer!

To forget to thank God for his many blessings is serious enough, but it is much worse to refuse to ask his help and his blessing on our endeavors or when we are in distress.

Asking the Lord's help is a way of manifesting our love for him and our trust in him.

Our gracious Father promised us: "When you call me, when you go to pray to me, I will listen to you." (Jer 29:12)

2 Psalm 5:2-3 I Will Listen
Hearken to my words, O Lord, / attend to my sighing. / Heed my call for help, / my king and my God!

Recognizing the Lord as our King and our God, we are also acknowledging our complete dependence upon him. We are, likewise, keeping ourselves aware of the truth that without him we can do nothing.

This pleases our Father immensely because then we are receptive to the help he wishes to give us. His infinite love for us compels him to make a loving response to our earnest pleading.

Jesus promised: " . . . all you ask the Father in my name, / he will give you." (Jn 15:16)

3 Psalm 17:6 Keep Asking
I call upon you, for you will answer me, O God; / incline your ear to me; hear my word.

A perplexing question naturally arises about our asking God for some favor or gift since he already knows all our needs and knows also what is good for us.

The Lord wants us to exercise our desire through prayer so that we may be able to receive what he is preparing to give us. His gifts are great, but our capacity is often limited and small. The deeper our faith, the stronger our hope, the greater our desire, the greater will be our capacity to receive whatever gift he wishes to give us.

Isaiah explains the need for asking and waiting: "No ear has ever heard, no eye ever seen, / any God but you / doing such deeds for those who wait for him." (Is 64:3)

4 Psalm 43:1-2a   Not of This World
Do me justice, O God, and fight my fight / against a faithless people; / from the deceitful and impious man rescue me. / For you, O God, are my strength.

We are living in the midst of "a faithless people." Our society is quite humanistic and materialistic. Its influence upon us personally is pernicious and subtle since we are not always aware of the erosion which is taking place within us. Gradually we find ourselves doubting or questioning our Christian way of life and its standards.

Spending some time each day with the Lord in prayer will help us maintain a healthy balance between the sacred and the sinful in our environment.

Jesus prayed for this: "I do not ask you to take them out of the world, / but to guard them from the evil one. / They are not of the world, / any more than I belong to the world." (Jn 17:15-16)

5 Psalm 43:3   Lead Kindly Light
Send forth your light and your fidelity; / they shall lead me on / and bring me to your holy mountain, / to your dwelling-place.

Light is the symbol of the presence of God. It is used frequently as an attribute of the Holy Spirit.

On our journey through life, the light of the Holy Spirit guides and enlightens us. In his fidelity the Holy Spirit is always abiding with us, supporting and strengthening us as we make our way to his holy mountain, to his dwelling-place.

Jesus promised us the guidance of the Holy Spirit: "The Paraclete, the Holy Spirit / whom the Father will send in my name, / will instruct you in everything, / and remind you of all that I told you." (Jn 14:26)

6 Psalm 118:5-6 Fear Not

In my straits I called upon the Lord; / the Lord answered me and set me free. / The Lord is with me; I fear not; / what can man do against me?

When we confidently implore the Lord, especially in difficulty, he will always respond, perhaps not in the way we wish, but he will grace us abundantly according to his divine plan for us. This reassurance will increase our faith and trust. What is more, it will remove all worry, fear, and anxiety from our hearts.

Listen to St. Paul's encouragement: "If God is for us, who can be against us?" (Rom 8:31)

7 Psalm 124:8 Frequent Reminder

Our help is in the name of the Lord, / who made heaven and earth.

We find this invocation introducing many of the prayers and blessings of the church. It is a sort of attitudinal adjustment prayer, reminding us that all our help comes from God and without him we are powerless.

We are also reminded that as Creator of the heavens and the earth, there is nothing in the realm of possibilities that he will not do for us if we are properly disposed to trust him and believe that he can and will come to our aid.

The beloved disciple tells us: "If our consciences have nothing to charge us with, / we can be sure that God is with us / and that we will receive at his hands / whatever we ask." (1 Jn 3:21f)

Power-Packed Prayer

The first seven verses of Psalm 86 form a perfect prayer of petition which God can hardly resist. The variety of petitions proves God's loving concern about every aspect of our life.

We should never stop asking because God, in his boundless love, cannot stop giving. Our asking also makes us more conscious of our total dependence on the Lord. It manifests our trust in him.

The psalmist teaches us another valuable lesson: appreciation, gratitude, and thankfulness for God's bountiful gifts. "I will give thanks to you, O Lord my God, / with all my heart, / and I will glorify your name forever." (Ps 86:12)

1 Psalm 86:1   Blessing in Disguise

Incline your ear, O Lord; answer me, / for I am afflicted and poor.

At times we are apt to consider human affliction, suffering, and sorrow as a punishment for sin. It is true that a life of dissipation may lead to physical illness, but this is due to our human condition.

God may use physical affliction to draw us closer to him, but he does not inflict it upon us as a vengeful punishment.

With the psalmist we too can plead for the Lord to incline his ear to us because of our affliction.

With the leper we can pray: "Lord, if you will to do so, you can cure me." (Lk 5:12)

2 Psalm 86:2   I Trust in You
Keep my life, for I am devoted to you; / save your servant who trusts in you.

We trust the people we love. We know that they have our welfare at heart. They will do everything in their power to bring us joy and happiness. Putting our trust in them is a great compliment to them.

Our prayer of petition is powerful when we ask fully trusting that the Lord will hear us. If we are willing to accept whatever God sends us, knowing that he wants only what is good for us, then we are placing our wholehearted trust in him.

Jesus repeatedly asked for trust in him: "Everything is possible to a man who trusts." (Mk 9:23)

3 Psalm 86:3   Have Pity on Me
You are my God; have pity on me, O Lord, / for to you I call all the day.

Our God is a God of compassion. He is eager and anxious to grant our prayer even before we ask. However, it is for our good that we "call all the day."

Repeating our prayer refines our petition and helps us see more clearly what we really need and prepares us to use that gift well.

Furthermore, our turning to God in prayer "all the day" keeps us more aware of his presence with us all through the day. It also reminds us that God alone is the source of all good.

St. James, the first Bishop of Jerusalem, reminds us: "Every worthwhile gift, every genuine benefit comes from above, descending from the Father. . . ." (Jas 1:17)

4 Psalm 86:4 My Spirit Rejoices
Gladden the soul of your servant, / for to you, O Lord, I lift up my soul.

In these words we ask God for that quiet, interior joy which gladdens our heart. Genuine Christian joy springs from our personal relationship with the Lord. When we keep ourselves aware that God loves us just as we are, and that he loves us regardless of what we have done, then we will be a happy person.

There is much joy not only in discerning God's will but also in striving to fulfill it to the best of our ability.

Then the Holy Spirit will gift us with genuine joy: "The fruit of the Spirit is love, joy, peace...." (Gal 5:22)

5 Psalm 86:5 Forgive Us Our Trespasses
For you, O Lord, are good and forgiving, / abounding in kindness to all who call upon you.

God's love for us is unwearied. With an enduring love he takes pity on us. He forgives us for his own sake and remembers our sins no more (Is 43:25), so overwhelming is his love for us.

The Father wants us to ask for forgiveness in order to keep our heart humble and contrite.

Jesus asks us to manifest this same kind of forgiving love to others: "If you forgive the faults of others, your heavenly Father will forgive you yours." (Mt 6:14)

6 Psalm 86:6   Listen and Attend
Hearken, O Lord, to my prayer / and attend to the sound of my pleading.

With the sacred writer we beg the Lord to hearken and attend to the sound of our pleading. In his word the Lord asks us repeatedly to listen.

As we listen we will more easily recognize the Lord's response to our petition. His response may be a clear insight into what he wants us to do. It may be a peaceful, even joyous, acceptance of what is happening in our life at the time. We need to listen to break through our preoccupation with self and be receptive to what the Lord is saying.

Jesus encourages us not only to listen but to put into practice what we hear. "Let everyone heed what he hears!" (Mt 13:9)

7 Psalm 86:7   Expectant Faith
In the day of my distress I call upon you, / for you will answer me.

Our trust manifests the level of faith with which we turn to God. The faith of expectancy pleases God no end. He can hardly resist when we express our petition with so much confidence.

In distress we are more conscious of our need for God's help. We are also more aware of his goodness which will never desert us in our need. A brief reflection on God's continuous fidelity in responding to our need will greatly augment our faith.

Jesus gives us reason for our unlimited trust in the Father: "If you, with all your sins, know how to give your children what is good, how much more will your heavenly Father give good things to anyone who asks him!" (Mt 7:11)

Supplication

Supplication is a much stronger word than petition. It usually implies that we are so desperate that we beg urgently and insistently for help in our distress.

In supplication we present our plea humbly and earnestly before the Lord when we are in dire need.

In spite of the urgency of our need, we ask submissively, beseeching and imploring God to come to our rescue.

In his loving care and concern, God always responds in some fashion to our pleading. He is our faithful Father. This week let us pray with the psalmist as he pleads his cause and ours before the Lord.

1 Psalm 13:2-4 Profitable Waiting

How long, O Lord? Will you utterly forget me? / How long will you hide your face from me? / How long shall I harbor sorrow in my soul, / grief in my heart day after day?

Waiting patiently on the Lord gives us an opportunity to beg the Lord to listen with compassion to our need. Like the psalmist our greatest need is for forgiveness.

Our prayer should be one of asking the Lord not to look on the wrong we might have done but instead to grant us his merciful compassion.

St. Peter encourages us with these words: "The Lord does not delay in keeping his promise— though some consider it 'delay.' Rather, he shows you generous patience, since he wants none to perish but all to come to repentance." (2 Pet 3:9)

2 Psalm 27:7-8   Familiar Call
Hear, O Lord, the sound of my call; / have pity on me, and answer me. / Of you my heart speaks; you my glance seeks; / your presence, O Lord, I seek.

Every voice has a distinctive tonality and timbre which helps us recognize a person even though we may not be able to see the person. We readily recognize the sound of the voice of someone who is well known to us.

In this prayer we ask God to listen to the sound of our call. This implies that the Lord will recognize us by the sound of our voice and will respond to our supplication.

Jesus assures us that he will recognize our voice: "The sheep hear his voice / as he calls his own by name / and leads them out." (Jn 10:3)

3 Psalm 116:1-2   Love Responds
I love the Lord because he has heard my voice in supplication, / Because he has inclined his ear to me the day I called.

We are precious to the Lord. He loves us with an enduring love. Love responds graciously and generously to the needs of the beloved, provided the beloved is receptive to that love.

Our prayer of petition to our Father is never in vain. He has "inclined his ear" to us because he loves us. He responds by giving us what he knows we need. He asks that we trust that he will do so. Jesus urges us: "Ask and you shall receive, / that your joy may be full." (Jn 16:24)

4 Psalm 119:170   To the Rescue
Let my supplication reach you; / rescue me according to your promise.

Supplication is more than a request. It is an earnest, and often a desperate, plea in time of need. In desperation the writer turns to God for help. He feels certain that God will rescue him because God is always faithful to his promises.

We have the same loving Father who is deeply concerned about our welfare. We can be certain that he will come to our rescue also when we reach out to him. That is his solemn promise.

When we begin to sink as Peter did while attempting to walk on the water, may we cry out: ". . . Lord, save me!" (Mt 14:30)

5 Psalm 130:1-2   Mired in Misery
Out of the depths I cry to you, O Lord; / Lord, hear my voice! / Let your ears be attentive to my voice in supplication.

This ardent prayer is the opening words of the sixth penitential psalm in the liturgy of the church. It is a cry of one in dire need begging to be saved from spiritual misery.

These words can be used as our cry for all the help we need to achieve our own salvation. We are asking the Lord to be attentive to our supplication and to redeem us. When our prayer becomes a constant one, it instills confidence in us. Likewise, our oft-repeated prayer purifies our desire and rids us of those attachments which may hinder our progress on the road to salvation. The angel promised: ". . . He (Jesus) will save his people from their sins." (Mt 1:21)

6 Psalm 140:7-8a Grace in Abundance

I say to the Lord, you are my God; / hearken, O Lord, to my voice in supplication. / O God, my Lord, my strength and my salvation.

St. Paul warns us that life in this world is a warfare. The evil one never relents. We are constantly bombarded with the subtle and clever machinations of the devil who would allure us away from the straight and narrow road leading to eternal happiness.

We are not facing the battle alone. The Lord is the source of our strength. Jesus not only redeemed us but continues to walk at our side to help us bridge every obstacle we may encounter.

He gives us this reassurance: "My grace is enough for you, for in weakness power reaches perfection." (2 Cor 12:9)

7 Psalm 28:6-7 Joyful Thanks

Blessed be the Lord, / for he has heard the sound of my pleading; / the Lord is my strength and my shield. / In him my heart trusts, and I find help; / then my heart exults, and with my song I give him thanks.

The psalmist shows us the way to relate to our loving Father. He put all his trust in the Lord and begged his help. He entreated the Lord who did not fail him. Immediately the psalmist blesses the Lord and thanks him for his gracious goodness to him.

What a model for us! This is a perfect pattern for our life—to plead, to trust, to exult, and to thank the Lord.

Join Jesus as he says: "Father, I thank you for having heard me. / I know that you always hear me. . . ." (Jn 11:41-42)

WEEK THIRTY-TWO
Praise and Petition

Prayer of petition can easily become self-centered. We often become rather narrow in our vision with undue concern about our own needs, plans, and projects. Nevertheless, it is true that prayers of petition do help us recognize our dependency upon the goodness of God.

On the other hand, when we praise God our prayer does become more God-centered. Our Father knows all our needs and he will respond to them when we praise him. Praise also makes petitions and intercessions more universal and more cosmic.

Let us praise God daily for responding so bountifully to all our needs.

1 Psalm 18:50 Only One
Therefore will I proclaim you, O Lord, among the nations / and I will sing praise to your name.

In our humanness we forget so easily. We take too much for granted. We are even oblivious of the myriad gifts and blessings of the Lord upon us each day. In their excitement of being healed, nine of the ten lepers even neglected to return to thank Jesus.

On the other hand, if we are faithful in proclaiming our praise and gratitude to the Lord for his goodness, we can ever so gently remind others of their privileged duty to thank our generous Father. By geometric progression the praises of the Lord will soon be sung "among the nations." May Jesus never say of us: "Were not all ten made whole? Where are the other nine?" (Lk 17:17)

159

2 Psalm 22:23-24a   People of Praise
I will proclaim your name to my brethren; / in the midst of the assembly I will praise you: / "You who fear the Lord, praise him."

When we begin to comprehend even in a small degree the might and majesty of God, our heart and lips reverberate with his praise.

Likewise, we cannot contain his greatness within ourselves. We need to share it. As we gather in liturgical assemblies, we add our voice to the great chorus of praise, honor, and glory arising heavenward. Filled with awe and wonder, we naturally reflect the peace and joy of our hearts to our brethren.

The Lord says to us also: "I have made you a light to the nations, a means of salvation to the ends of the earth." (Acts 13:47)

3 Psalm 51:17   Teach Us to Pray
O Lord, open my lips, / and my mouth shall proclaim your praise.

This short verse is a fervent prayer of petition begging God to grace us with the gift of authentic prayer issuing from a humble, contrite heart. When our hearts are filled with wonder and reverence, when they overflow with joy and gratitude, then our prayer is pleasing to God.

These dispositions of mind and heart will lead us into proclaiming the praises of the Lord always and everywhere, under any and all circumstances.

Jesus advises us: "Your light must shine before men so that they may see goodness in your acts and give praise to your heavenly Father." (Mt 5:16)

4 **Psalm 66:16-17   Petitioning Is Praising**
Hear now, all you who fear God, while I declare what he has done for me. / When I appealed to him in words, / praise was on the tip of my tongue.

In these words the sacred writer reminds us of an ideal approach to God in prayer. Even though he was begging the Lord for a special favor, he says: "praise was on the tip of my tongue."

Praise is perfect prayer. God enjoys our praise because it establishes our relationship with him as creature to Creator. We readily fall into the habit of petitioning God and less frequently into praising him.

St. Paul is right on target when he says: "May the God of our Lord Jesus Christ, the Father of glory, grant you a spirit of wisdom and insight to know him clearly." (Eph 1:17)

5 **Psalm 76:5   His Sovereign Majesty**
Resplendent you came, O powerful One, / from the everlasting mountains.

This response of praise to our benevolent Father arises within us when we pause to consider how generously and graciously God has listened and granted our many petitions placed before him.

Extolling the Lord's power comes naturally to a grateful heart that has experienced the goodness and kindness of the Lord.

When our attention is drawn to a huge mountain, we immediately visualize the might and power of God whose dwelling place to the Hebrews was on the top of the mountain.

The three favorite apostles experienced the splendor of the Lord: "He was transfigured before their eyes. His face became as dazzling as the sun, his clothes as radiant as light." (Mt 17:2)

6 Psalm 109:30-31   Triumph Train
I speak my thanks earnestly to the Lord, / and in the midst of the throng I will praise him, / For he stood at the right hand of the poor man, / to save him from those who would condemn him.

The sacred writer witnessed the Lord's fidelity as "he stood at the right hand of the poor man." For such devoted fidelity, he thanks God earnestly.

As we pause to count our blessings we may be astounded at the beneficence of our loving Father. Our hearts, too, will yearn to thank God earnestly. Verbalizing our earnest thanks publicly as well as privately will enhance our own appreciation and draw others into a deeper sense of gratitude.

How encouragingly St. Paul reminds us of our ministry: "Thanks be to God, who unfailingly leads us on in Christ's triumphal train, and employs us to diffuse the fragrance of his knowledge everywhere! We are an aroma of Christ for God's sake." (2 Cor 2:14-15)

7 Psalm 115:12a-13   Boundless Blessings
The Lord remembers us and will bless us: / . . . He will bless those who fear the Lord, / both the small and the great.

The word "bless" embraces all God's special gifts. He wants to confer his blessings generously, but he does respect our freedom. If we fear him, that is, reverence him, we keep ourselves receptive to him. If we use his gifts well, he will be even more generous. God is not a respecter of persons. He loves "both the small and the great."

Sirach's words are right to the point: "Send up the sweet odor of your hymn of praise; / bless the Lord for all he has done! / Proclaim the greatness of his name, / loudly sing his praises." (Sir 39:14-15)

Part IX

Proclaim the Kingdom of God.
(Lk 9:60)

Father and King

In our times we are not accustomed to kings, queens, royal families, and all the pageantry which accompanies them. History does not portray all those wearing crowns and scepters as benign monarchs, to say the least.

However, when we call our loving Father a King, we are not speaking about an earthly kingdom. His kingdom is a kingdom of love. His power is love.

His creative love fashioned a universe with a special planet, earth, which we call home. His love continues to supply all our daily needs.

He is eagerly waiting to welcome us into his eternal kingdom where we will enjoy all the love, peace, and joy we can imagine. Let us reflect on the wonders of that kingdom!

1 Psalm 47:2-3   Kingly Father
All you peoples, clap your hands, / shout to God with cries of gladness, / For the Lord, the Most High, the awesome, / is the great king over all the earth.

God is King of all the earth. He is Lord of all creation. He is our King and also our Father. We are his adopted sons and daughters. We belong to his royal family.

God's reign of love began in us as a tiny mustard seed when he came to make his dwelling place with us at the moment of our baptism. This gives us our true dignity as persons and Christians. With the saints we pray: "We praise you, the Lord God Almighty, / who is and who was. / You have assumed your great power, / you have begun your reign." (Rev 11:17)

2 Psalm 47:8-9   Power of Love
For the king of all the earth is God; / sing hymns of praise. / God reigns over the nations, / God sits upon his holy throne.

God is a mighty King. He is supreme. His power is beyond compare. His power is love.

Love must give. Love must be translated into action. Love elicits a response. Love asks a commitment. Can we say no to love?

With the heavenly hosts let us sing: "Alleluia! / The Lord is king, / our God, the Almighty! / Let us rejoice and be glad, / and give him glory!" (Rev 19:6f)

3 Psalm 74:12 and 16-17   Chorus of Praise
Yet, O God, my king from of old, / you doer of saving deeds on earth .... Yours is the day, and yours the night; / you fashioned the moon and the sun. / You fixed all the limits of the land; / summer and winter you made.

Inanimate creation rejoices as it welcomes its King. Stand on the beach and listen as the waves of the sea roll up to your feet thundering the praises of God.

Listen to the cascading waves splashing amid the rocks, clapping their hands with joy. Listen as the mountains reverberate with praise re-echoing through the valleys. The sun and moon light up all the beauty of creation and nurture it to fruition. "God looked at everything he had made, and he found it very good." (Gen 1:31)

4 Psalm 84:4 My King and My God
Even the sparrow finds a home, / and the swallow a nest / in which she puts her young — / Your altars, O Lord of hosts, / my king and my God!

The Lord is my King and my God! He is also the King of the sparrow, the swallow, and all the birds of the air, all of which he created and cares for.

God created the birds for our benefit. We cherish their melodious song. We enjoy the beauty of their plumage. Some species even provide food for our nourishment.

How comforting the words of Jesus: "Look at the birds in the sky. They do not sow or reap, they gather nothing into barns; yet your heavenly Father feeds them. Are not you more important than they?" (Mt. 6:26)

5 Psalm 93:1 King of Creation
The Lord is king, in spendor robed; / robed is the Lord and girt about with strength; / And he has made the world firm, / not to be moved.

Pope St. Clement writes: "Let us fix our gaze on the Father and Creator of the whole world.

"By his direction the heavens are in motion, and they are subject to him in peace. Day and night fulfill the course he has established without interfering with each other. The sun, the moon, and the choirs of stars revolve in harmony at his command in their appointed paths and without deviation. By his will the earth blossoms in the proper seasons and produces abundant food for men and animals and all living things on it without reluctance and without violation of what he has arranged."

Jesus proclaimed his kingship: "You will see the Son of Man seated at the right hand of the Power and coming with the clouds of heaven." (Mk 14:62)

6 **Psalm 98:8-9   Give Him the Glory**
Let the rivers clap their hands, / the mountains shout with them for joy / Before the Lord, for he comes, / for he comes to rule the earth.

The psalmist paints a comprehensive picture in poetic imagery of all creation joyously praising God. We can well imagine the rivers clapping their hands and the mountains shouting for joy. What a tremendous outburst of joy and praise this would be!

As we contemplate such a picture in our minds, our hearts dance with joy. We want to join the full orchestra of nature and men in praising God.

Let us join the great crowd in John's vision: "The Lord is king, / our God, the Almighty! / Let us rejoice and be glad, / and give him glory!" (Rev 19:6f)

7 **Psalm 45:2   Lilting Praise**
My heart overflows with a goodly theme; / as I sing my ode to the king, / my tongue is nimble as the pen of a skillful scribe.

Even a brief reflection on the wonders of God's creative love surrounding us on all sides fills our heart with awe and reverence. As our reflection carries us into the realization that all of this was created for our need and enjoyment, our heart responds with gratitude and joy.

As our heart overflows with praise, our tongue sings out the praises of the Lord.

Let us sing our praises with the sacred writer: "Mighty and wonderful are your works, / Lord God Almighty! / Righteous and true are your ways, / O King of the nations!" (Rev 15:3)

Jesus Our King

Our heavenly Father is our King. He loves us so much that he gave us his only Son as our Savior and Redeemer. Jesus, too, is our King. His rule is also a rule of love.

His redemptive love brought him to the cross, conferring on us our adoption as sons and daughters of the Father. This adoption made us members of the royal family. As Christians we are blue bloods in the real sense of the term. God is our Father, Jesus is our Brother.

The only submission which Jesus asks of us as his subjects is our love in return for the boundless love he has already and will continue to pour out upon us.

Let us join the psalmist in singing the praises of the Lord.

1 Psalm 24:9-10   A Receptive Heart
Lift up, O gates, your lintels; / reach up, you ancient portals, / that the king of glory may come in! / Who is this king of glory? / The Lord of hosts; he is the king of glory.

The Lord wants to establish his kingdom in our hearts. He will never force himself upon us. He waits to be invited. The psalmist encourages us to lift the gates of our hearts to receive him.

At every Mass the celebrant introduces the Lord's Prayer with these words: "Let us pray for the coming of the kingdom as Jesus taught us."

Jesus urges us to condition our lives to permit his kingdom to be formed in us. Listen to Jesus' own words: "Reform your lives! The kingdom of heaven is at hand." (Mt 4:17)

2 Psalm 98:4 and 6   Thy Kingdom Come
Sing joyfully to the Lord, all you lands; / break into song; sing praise. . . . / With trumpets and the sound of the horn / sing joyfully before the King, the Lord.

Jesus established his kingdom by his redemptive death and glorious resurrection. However, his kingdom of love is not fully established in the hearts of all people. That is why we pray at Mass for the coming of his kingdom in the Lord's prayer: "Thy kingdom come." His kingdom should rule in every human heart.

Our mission in life is to radiate the joy which his kingdom brings with it. Joy is contagious. It draws others to itself. This is the Lord's special gift to us.

Jesus advises us: "The gift you have received, give as a gift." (Mt 10:8)

3 Psalm 97:1-2   Universal Kingdom
The Lord is king; let the earth rejoice / let the many isles be glad. / Clouds and darkness are round about him, / justice and judgment are the foundation of his throne.

God's kingdom is a universal kingdom embracing all peoples from many isles. It is also an enduring kingdom because it is a kingdom of love. Every human heart longs to be loved.

As Victor Herbert sang: "It is love and love alone which makes the world go round." That love rains down upon us from the throne of our King and God.

St. John relates: "The Word became flesh / and made his dwelling among us, / and we have seen his glory: / the glory of an only Son coming from the Father, / filled with enduring love." (Jn 1:14)

4 Psalm 145:1-2   My God and King
I will extol you, O my God and King, / and I will bless your name forever and ever. / Every day will I bless you, / and I will praise your name forever and ever.

In this prayer we promise our God and King that we will extol, bless, and praise him forever. This is our firm commitment to him as our gracious Father and sovereign King.

There is also a prayer of petition implied herein. If we are to praise and glorify God "forever and ever," then we are begging him to bring us into the eternal happiness of heaven so that we may continue to praise, bless, and extol his name forever and ever.

St. Paul's doxology is brief but fervent: "Blessed forever be God who is over all! Amen." (Rom 9:5)

5 Psalm 99:1 and 3   Not of This World
The Lord is king; the peoples tremble; / he is throned upon the cherubim; the earth quakes. . . . / Let them praise your great and awesome name; / holy is he!

God is the transcendent King of heaven and earth. His is a kingdom ruled by love.

Even though his kingdom is not of this world, he devised a way and means whereby we could become members of his kingdom even during our earthly existence. Through baptism we become members of his royal family. He shares his divine life with us partially in this life but in all its fullness in the life to come.

Jesus explained the nature of his kingdom: "My kingdom does not belong to this world. . . . / my kingdom is not here." (Jn 18:36)

6 **Psalm 145:12-13   Community of Love**
Making known to men your might / and the glorious splendor of your kingdom. / Your kingdom is a kingdom for all ages, / and your dominion endures through all generations.

When we speak of love, we use expressions which give it the luster of eternity. Love lasts forever. It is not transitory. If this is the quality we expect in human love, how much more do we find it in divine love.

God established his kingdom as a community of love. He formed it as a family living in peace and love, in harmony and heavenly accord. Love is eternal and since God's kingdom is a reign of love, it, too, "endures through all generations."

St. James asks us a pertinent question: "Did not God choose those who are poor in the eyes of the world to be rich in faith and heirs of the kingdom he promised to those who love him?" (Jas 2:5)

7 **Psalm 47:6-7   Our Enthroned King**
God mounts his throne amid shouts of joy; / the Lord, amid trumpet blasts. / Sing praise to God, sing praise; / sing praise to our king, sing praise.

This psalm describes accurately the ascension of Jesus into heaven. In his glorified body, Jesus has gone beyond time and space. The ascension of Jesus is our glory and our joy. By his power we will follow him into glory.

Our joy at this prospect is best expressed in praise. Our praise must be voiced. It must resound and reverberate from our hearts.

St. Paul's solicitude is well detected: "Since you have been raised up in company with Christ, set your heart on what pertains to higher realms where Christ is seated at God's right hand. Be intent on things above rather than on things of earth." (Col 3:1-2)

Kingdom of Peace

There is a wide range of meaning to the word "peace" as it is used in modern parlance. The *shalom* spoken by Jesus means a tranquillity of mind and heart in the face of spiritual or temporal trials leading us to the joy of heaven.

God is the author and dispenser of that interior, spiritual, free gift we call peace. It is one of the fruits of the Holy Spirit dwelling in our hearts.

Peace is one of the most comprehensive and highly-prized gifts of God. It is the crowning blessing of the Messianic age. In fact, it belongs to the very essence of the Messianic kingdom.

We enjoy genuine peace when we are at peace with God, with ourselves, with our neighbor, and with nature.

1 Psalm 85:9   Peace with God

I will hear what God proclaims; / the Lord—for he proclaims peace. / To his people, and to his faithful ones, / and to those who put in him their hope.

The first great source of peace springs from our relationship with God, our loving Father. When our will is attuned to God's will, especially his will of preference, then we will be "his faithful ones." We will then enjoy that unique peace which only God can give.

When we recognize the Father's love for us as he recreates us, provides for us, forgives us, consoles us, and continues to love us with an enduring love, then we will experience a genuine peace.

The Holy Spirit assures us: "Now that we have been justified by faith, we are at peace with God through our Lord Jesus Christ." (Rom 5:1)

2 Psalm 119:165-166   Peace with Self

Those who love your law have great peace, / and for them there is no stumbling block. / I wait for your salvation, O Lord, / and your commands I fulfill.

The Lord knows our humanness and how prone we are to turn away from him occasionally to follow our own will.

Jesus assures us that he is aware of our disloyalty, yet he will never abandon us, nor should our sinfulness cause us to be discouraged or even to despair. "I tell you all this / that in me you may find peace." (Jn 16:33)

3 Psalm 122:7-8   Peace with One Another

May peace be within your walls, / prosperity in your buildings. / Because of my relatives and friends / I will say, "Peace be within you!"

Every person is our brother or sister since we are all the temples of the Holy Spirit. We are all members of God's family since we have a common Father who adopted us as his daughters and sons.

Our acceptance of one another brings us much peace. Scripture reminds us: "The kingdom of God is not a matter of eating or drinking, but of justice, peace, and the joy that is given by the Holy Spirit. Whoever serves Christ in this way pleases God and wins the esteem of men. Let us, then, make it our aim to work for peace and to strengthen one another." (Rom 14:17-19)

4 Psalm 147:14-15   Peace in Nature

He has granted peace in your borders; / with the best of wheat he fills you. / He sends forth his command to the earth; / swiftly runs his word!

We are at peace with nature when we accept whatever climatic conditions prevail. We happily adjust to heat or cold, to rain or sunshine. We do not permit even dark overcast skies to depress us.

We are at peace with nature when we enjoy the beauty and grandeur of God's creation around us and use these created gifts as God intended.

As the Prince of Peace Jesus brings: "Glory to God in high heaven, / peace on earth to those on whom his favor rests." (Lk 2:14)

5 Psalm 29:10-11   Peace

The Lord is enthroned above the flood; / the Lord is enthroned as king forever. / May the Lord give strength to his people; / may the Lord bless his people with peace.

God our Father established his kingdom as a reign of peace. Jesus is the Prince of Peace and the Holy Spirit is the very source of peace.

In his kindness God sent us his Son Jesus: "To shine on those who sit in darkness and / in the shadow of death, / to guide our feet into the way of peace." (Lk 1:79)

6 Psalm 72:3 and 7
Peace an Enduring Gift

The mountains shall yield peace for the people, / and the hills justice. / Justice shall flower in his days, / and profound peace, till the moon be no more.

The psalmist often refers to mountain peaks and hill tops as the abiding place of God. From this vantage point he pictures God, the source of all peace, pouring out his peace upon his people.

The peace of mind and heart which the Lord gives is an abiding gift "till the moon be no more." Such peace is the foretaste of the eternal peace of heaven.

From the heights of Calvary such peace flows down to us: "It pleased God to make absolute fullness reside in him and by means of him, to reconcile everything in his person, both on earth and in the heavens, making peace through the blood of his cross." (Col 1:19-20)

7 Psalm 37:11 Eternal Peace

But the meek shall possess the land, / they shall delight in abounding peace.

A meek person endures injury with patience and without resentment, nor does he seek revenge. To live this way of life is difficult at times, but its fruits are abundant.

When we practice this attitude of meekness, we will discover great strength and an interior joy which no one can take from us. Jesus promised us great peace not only in this life but the eternal peace of heaven, which is what is meant by the expression "shall possess the land."

Jesus' gratuitous blessing: "'Peace' is my farewell to you, / my peace is my gift to you; / I do not give it to you as the world gives peace." (Jn 14:27)

Kingdom of Love

Today, kings and queens and royal pageantry are scarcely known. This fact may hamper our appreciation of the kingdom of God.

Jesus explained that his kingdom is not of this world. It is a kingdom of love. God is love, and he shares that part of his nature with us even in this life but more fully when we enter into his kingdom. Heaven is his kingdom—a state of perfect happiness.

Since at baptism we become members of his kingdom, our eternal destiny is heaven, a community of perfect love.

What joy, what praise arises in our hearts as we focus on the kingdom which awaits us.

1 Psalm 8:3 Perfect Praise
Out of the mouths of babes and sucklings / you have fashioned praise because of your foes, / to silence the hostile and the vengeful.

God created us in his own image, thus making us the greatest of all his creatures. God gave us a share in his own dominion. Our real greatness, however, lies in the fact that we can recognize God as our sovereign Lord. We are greater than the stars because we can praise God.

Yet we stand before the Eternal as a child. Our praise is pleasing to God when it is childlike—simple and unassuming. Jesus warrants our praise because: "He has put all things under Christ's feet and has made him, thus exalted, head of the church, which is his body: the fullness of him who fills the universe in all its parts." (Eph 1:22-23)

2 Psalm 68:5 Exultation
Sing to God, chant praise to his name, / extol him who rides upon the clouds, / Whose name is the Lord; / exult before him.

The image of God riding upon the clouds conveys the notion of his transcendence. It is an ancient epithet for God. Likewise, "whose name is the Lord" is a recognition of all his divine attributes.

As the sovereign Lord and Master of the heavens, he deserves our praise.

In his final blessing upon his people, Moses emphasizes God's divinity: "There is no god like the God of the darling, / who rides the heavens in his power, / and rides the skies in his majesty." (Dt 33:26)

3 Psalm 96:4-5 No Other God
For great is the Lord and highly to be praised; / awesome is he, beyond all gods. / For all the gods of the nations are things of nought, / but the Lord made the heavens.

In these verses of the psalm we are invited to praise the "Lord who made the heavens" as the only Lord and Master in our lives. This admonition is always timely. Other gods can easily take priority in our lives without our being aware of it.

The neon gods of self-centeredness, pride, and pleasure loom up frequently in our daily living. Another god clamoring for attention and acceptance is the plastic god of escapism, be it into pleasure, hyperactivity, or chemical dependency. As we faithfully praise the Lord who made the heavens, we need no other god.

The Father announced the divinity of Jesus when he said at the baptism of Jesus: "This is my beloved Son. My favor rests on him." (Mt 3:17)

4 Psalm 96:6-7 Majestic Splendor

Splendor and majesty go before him; / praise and grandeur are in his sanctuary. / Give to the Lord, you families of nations, / give to the Lord glory and praise; / give to the Lord the glory due his name!

Shakespeare has Hamlet say: "Words, words, words!" When we try to comprehend God, or try to describe some aspect of the Lord, we, too, are tempted to say the same. No words have even been coined to relate the experience of God, or describe his fidelity, beauty, or love. "Splendor, majesty, and grandeur" are magnificent words, but even these are inadequate to convey some idea of God.

In our inadequacy we can only say with the psalmist: "Give to the Lord glory and praise; / give to the Lord the glory due his name!"

5 Psalm 145:21 Look to Him

May my mouth speak the praise of the Lord, / and may all flesh bless his holy name forever and ever.

The dominant thought of this hymn is the Lord's greatness, especially his sovereign majesty and loving providence. We ask that we may praise the Lord so that we may concentrate more on the person of God rather than on his gifts.

We are conscious of our own inadequacy in offering the Lord the praise which is his due; hence we pray that all creatures "bless his holy name forever and ever."

St. Paul's pastoral advice is brief but direct: "Give thanks to God the Father always and for everything in the name of our Lord Jesus Christ." (Eph 5:20)

6 Psalm 146:1-2   Praise the Lord
Praise the Lord, O my soul; / I will praise the Lord all my life; / I will sing praise to my God while I live.

As we try to behold God, our hearts are moved to lift our voices in praising him. Praise is theocentric. In praising God we can easily become lost in his presence.

Praise leads us into adoration. It is conducive to contemplation and even ecstasy. Let us pray: "Praise the Lord, O my soul."

St. Paul's admonition is filled with joy: "Be filled with the Spirit, addressing one another in psalms and hymns and inspired songs. Sing praise to the Lord with all your hearts." (Eph 5:18b-19)

7 Psalm 147:12-13   New Jerusalem
Glorify the Lord, O Jerusalem; / praise your God, O Zion. / For he has strengthened the bars of your gates; / he has blessed your children within you.

We are the new Jerusalem—the kingdom of God within us. We are Zion, the people of God. We are invited to glorify the Lord simply because he is God.

As we praise and glorify God, joy floods our soul. We manifest our joy by a cheerful countenance, a loving concern for others, the sheer excitement of daily living in the midst of God's beautiful creation. Our spirit of joy is contagious. And St. John confirms that the new Jerusalem awaits us: "This is God's dwelling among men. He shall dwell with them and they shall be his people and he shall be their God who is always with them." (Rev 21:3)

Part X

God of All Consolation

(2 Cor 1:3)

Hope Equals Happiness

Faith, hope, and charity are called the theological virtues because they have God as their object and they keep our focus centered on God.

The virtue of hope is an attitude of confident expectancy and firm trust in God. It is yearning for that final union with God in love.

Hope helps us recognize that God is real, that he loves us with an enduring love, and that he is always faithful to all his promises.

Hope creates within us a desire for God and a longing to be closely united with him. Hope enables us to see everything in the light of eternity.

May the following days of prayer this week increase and strengthen our hope.

1 Psalm 62:6-7   Only in God

Only in God be at rest, my soul, / for from him comes my hope. / He only is my rock and my salvation, / my stronghold; I shall not be disturbed.

God, our loving Father, is the only genuine source of hope for us on our pilgrim's way. The psalmist uses the word "only" to impress upon us that all our hope should reside in God.

He also calls God "rock" to indicate the solid foundation upon which we have placed all our hope. This foundation is opposed to human help which is illusory. Jesus impresses us with the solidity of his word as a firm foundation: "Anyone who hears my words and puts them into practice is like the wise man who built his house on rock." (Mt 7:24)

2 Psalm 31:25 Hope Gives Strength
Take courage and be stouthearted, / all you who hope in the Lord.

Hope generates in us an expectation of the happiness and peace which awaits us in the future life. Hope makes us stouthearted because it brings with it a real dynamism to live our life according to God's plan regardless of the opposition.

Hope enables us to take courage as it strengthens us for the constant combat along life's path. The allurements and the temptations of the evil one are always present.

St. Paul's words are encouraging: "The grace of God has appeared, offering salvation to all men. It trains us to reject godless ways and worldly desires, and live temperately, justly, and devoutly in this age as we await our blessed hope, the appearing of the glory of the great God and of our Savior Christ Jesus." (Ti 2:11-13)

3 Psalm 33:22 Mercy Sparks Hope
May your kindness, O Lord, be upon us / who have put our hope in you.

The virtue of hope enables us to put our whole life into God's hands. It keeps us aware that God not only forgives our sins but he also turns every misfortune and suffering to our eternal advantage. Nothing is endured in vain. Nor do we need to be unduly concerned about our faults and failures. When we come before the Lord with all our sins, he can draw some good from it by helping us grow in humility and in our dependence upon him. Let us pray with St. Paul: "May our Lord Jesus Christ himself, may God our Father who loved us and in his mercy gave us eternal consolation and hope, console your hearts and strengthen them for every good work and word." (2 Thes 2:16-17)

4 Psalm 42:6b   Rejoice in Hope
Hope in God! For I shall again be thanking him, / in the presence of my savior and my God.

As we recall and thank God for his countless blessings upon us moment by moment, we become more deeply aware of his concerned, caring love for each one of us.

This awareness stimulates an ardent hope within us and produces an unshakable trust in our loving Father.

In his pastoral concern, St. Paul advises us: "Rejoice in hope, be patient under trial, persevere in prayer." (Rom 12:12)

5 Psalm 119:116   God's Gift
Sustain me as you have promised, that I may live; / disappoint me not in my hope.

Hope is a gift from God. Like every gift we must not only willingly accept it but use that gift thus permitting it to grow and mature within us. The way to cause hope to grow within us is to pray daily for an increase of hope. We ought to pray confidently and expectantly that hope will characterize our daily living.

We need to pray that God's gift of hope will sustain us in times of trial and temptation, in times of suffering both physical and mental. Hope wards off every tinge of discouragement.

St. Paul prays with us and for us: "So may God, the source of hope, fill you with all joy and peace in believing so that through the power of the Holy Spirit you may have hope in abundance." (Rom 15:13)

6 Psalm 146:5   Joy in Hope
Happy he whose help is the God of Jacob, / whose hope is in the Lord, his God.

Hope keeps us patient in trials and difficulties. Hope makes us joyful Christians even in times of suffering and pain.

Let us reflect on the advice St. Peter gives us: "Do not be surprised, beloved, that a trial by fire is occurring in your midst. It is a test for you, but it should not catch you off guard. Rejoice instead, in the measure that you share Christ's sufferings. When his glory is revealed, you will rejoice exultantly." (1 Pt 4:12-13)

7 Psalm 147:11   No Worry
The Lord is pleased with those who fear him, / with those who hope for his kindness.

In today's world the tensions, anxieties, insecurity, crimes, war, and the suffering of the innocent could very readily lead us into discouragement and even into bitterness. We need a joyful hope.

Genuine hope looks beyond the confines of our terrestrial existence to the glory of a life hereafter. All hope must have this eternal dimension. Hope gives us the expectation and yearning for what we know will be awaiting us when we reach our home in heaven.

St. Peter's advice is worth recalling: "Bow humbly under God's mighty hand, so that in due time he may lift you high. Cast all your cares on him because he cares for you." (1 Pt 5:6-7)

Our Family

God's love is fathomless. It is enduring. It is incomprehensible. One aspect of his kindness is the unique love which God has implanted in the human family.

A family is united not only by blood ties but by a special bond of love. We often speak of a family as a miniature church since it is a community of love where we first learned about God's love for us.

Make this a thanskgiving week for your family. Let us pause to appreciate our own family and also to thank God for permitting us to be a member of our own special family. Thank God for mother and father, for brothers and sisters, and for all our friends and relatives.

1 Psalm 66:8-9 Life a Divine Gift
Bless our God, you peoples, / loudly sound his praise; / He has given life to our souls, / and has not let our feet slip.

One of the many mysteries of life is God's creative power. We are the wonder of his creation. Love must share; hence God shared his creative power with men and women. Through their mutual love, husband and wife manifest the awesomeness of God's unfathomable love in creating a life that will never end.

As we reflect on God's creative love, joy and gratitude fill our hearts to overflowing for the gift of life so freely given.

We are the masterpiece of his creation since: "God created man in his image; / in the divine image he created him; / male and female he created them." (Gn 1:27)

187

2 Psalm 9:2 My Mother, Your Mother
I will give thanks to you, O Lord, with all my heart; / I will declare all your wondrous deeds. / I will be glad and exult in you; / I will sing praise to your name, Most High.

Today let us thank God for the gift of our own mother. Ask God to bless her, living or dead, for all the loving care and concern she gave us. Beg him to heal her for the worry and anxiety we might have caused her.

Jesus gave us his Mother as our very own also, to challenge and edify us along the road of life.

With what pain and joy Jesus must have said: "There is your son. . . . There is your mother." (Jn 19:26-27)

3 Psalm 75:2 Faithful Fathers
We give you thanks, O God, we give thanks, / and we invoke your name; we declare your wondrous deeds.

Fatherhood is one of God's "wondrous deeds." Make this day Father's Day in your prayer. May our prayer be one of heartfelt thanks and gratitude for our own father and for all the faithful fathers in our land.

Recall the countless sacrifices which our fathers have made to protect and provide for us, to educate and encourage us, and above all to love us.

Jesus pays a great tribute to fathers when he speaks of his heavenly Father! "Would one of you [fathers] hand his son a stone when he asks for a loaf?" (Mt 7:9)

4 Psalm 133:1
Brother Love—Love One Another

Behold, how good it is, and how pleasant, / where brethren dwell as one!

Since our human nature is wounded by sinfulness, it is likely that little misunderstandings and disagreements may arise in a family. Genuine love surmounts all these differences.

Christian love helps us to accept each other as brothers and sisters with all our faults and foibles. Such acceptance causes our love to grow and mature. It also brings much peace and happiness into a family.

Sirach says these are worthy of praise: "With three things I am delighted, / for they are pleasing to the Lord and to men: / Harmony among brethren, friendship among neighbors, / and the mutual love of husband and wife." (Sir 25:1)

5 Psalm 30:5 Grandparents Are Special

Sing praise to the Lord, you his faithful ones, / and give thanks to his holy name.

Grandparents are very special people. They lavish so many kindnesses upon us. They are proud of us. They make us proud of ourselves. They give us a feeling of being loved and accepted beyond our immediate family.

Grandparents also give us a sense of our roots, enabling us to accept ourselves and be proud of our heritage. We are grateful to God for all that he has given us, but today let us thank him especially for our grandparents.

St. Paul's words are strong: "If anyone does not provide for his own relatives and especially for members of his immediate family, he has denied the faith; he is worse than an unbeliever." (1 Tm 5:8)

6 Psalm 145:10-11   Big Family

Let all your works give you thanks, O Lord, / and let your faithful ones bless you. / Let them discourse of the glory of your kingdom / and speak of your might.

Most of us have an extended family—uncles and aunts, cousins and distant relatives galore. In our extended family, God, in his providential love, has given us some very special people.

These relatives give us a sense of belonging. Their caring attitude makes us loved and accepted. It gives us a wholesome sense of our importance.

How very good is the Lord who has surrounded us with the loving care and concern which so many relatives lavish upon us! "Her neighbors and relatives, upon hearing that the Lord had extended his mercy to her, rejoiced with her." (Lk 1:58)

7 Psalm 57:10-11   Friendship

I will give thanks to you among the peoples, O Lord, / I will chant your praise among the nations, / For your kindness towers to the heavens, / and your faithfulness to the skies.

Friends are just another one of God's manifold gifts to us. We are social beings. We depend on others. We need to share with others.

Real friends accept us as we are. We have no need for pretending. We can relax with them and be ourselves. Sirach says: "A faithful friend is a sturdy shelter; / he who finds one finds a treasure. / A faithful friend is beyond price, / no sum can balance his worth." (Sir 6:14-15)

Our Spiritual Family

The name 'angel' does not indicate so much the nature of these angelic beings but rather their function as messengers of the Lord. We learn about them primarily through their ministry.

The angels are helpers of Jesus in his salvific work (Heb 1:14). They protect and guide us (Mt 18:10).They present to God the prayer of the faithful (Rev 8:3). They lead the souls of the just into paradise (Lk 16:22). They protect the church, the body of Christ (Rev 12:7-9).

The angels are another manifestation of God's provident love. As we contemplate the angels, we are moved to thank them for their devoted service and beg them to continue hovering over us at all times.

1 Psalm 8:6 Pure Spirit

You have made him little less than the angels, / and crowned him with glory and honor.

Man is the masterpiece of God's creation on earth. God created man in his own image and likeness. He gave him dominion over all creation.

Though God so richly endowed man, he is still a "little less than the angels." Angels are pure spirits surrounding the throne of God, praising and glorifying God with an endless hymn of praise.

The sacred writer speaks of Jesus' humanity in these words: ". . . we do see Jesus crowned with glory and honor because he suffered death: Jesus, who was made for a little while lower than the angels, that through God's gracious will he might taste death for the sake of all men." (Heb 2:9)

2 Psalm 103:20-21   Angels Lead the Way
Bless the Lord, all you his angels / you mighty in strength, who do his bidding, / obeying his spoken word. / Bless the Lord, all you his hosts, / his ministers, who do his will.

The angels are not only our guardians and companions during our earthly exile but they also challenge us by their own example.

They do the bidding of the Lord at all times; they obey his spoken word; they do his will. They bless the Lord with us and for us. They inspire and encourage us to follow their lead so that we may praise and glorify God for all eternity with them.

The angels carried out the message that the Lord gave them: "You have nothing to fear! I come to proclaim good news to you—tidings of great joy to be shared by the whole people. This day in David's city a savior has been born to you, the Messiah and Lord." (Lk 2:10-11)

3 Psalm 91:11-12   Guard Duty
For to his angels he has given command about you, / that they guard you in all your ways. / Upon their hands they shall bear you up, / lest you dash your foot against a stone.

God's caring and concerned love overshadows us at every moment of our existence. Such love is simply too great for us to comprehend.

One of the expressions of his caring love is the creation of angels as our special companions in life. The angels shield and protect us from harm. They inspire and encourage us. They bear us up and lead us on our journey back to the Father.

Tobit's prayer can easily be our prayer: "May God in heaven protect you on the way and bring you back to me safe and sound; and may his angel accompany you for safety." (Tob 5:17)

4 Psalm 35:5-6 Angelic Protection

Let them be like chaff before the wind, / with the angel of the Lord driving them on. / Let their way be dark and slippery, / with the angel of the Lord pursuing them.

Using the imagery of the threshing floor, the psalmist prays that all danger be blown away like worthless chaff. He prays, too, that the angel of the Lord continue his pursuit of evil even though the way is dark and slippery.

As we pray for help and relief in times of trouble and affliction, we have the assurance that the protecting angels will ward off any threat of danger. This is the God-given mission.

Jesus warned us about caring for his little ones: "See that you never despise one of these little ones. I assure you, their angels in heaven constantly behold my heavenly Father's face." (Mt 18:10)

5 Psalm 34:8 Vigilant Companions

The angel of the Lord encamps / around those who fear him, and delivers them.

Here we have another image portraying the protective, providential love of the Lord. The angel of the Lord, which may mean the Lord himself, is with us at all times. His encamping signifies the permanency of his presence with us.

The disposition required of us is to believe in his boundless love and to trust wholeheartedly in his promise. Such faith and confidence ensures our deliverance from all impending evil.

God provides for our need: "See, I am sending an angel before you, to guard you on the way and bring you to the place I have prepared. Be attentive to him and heed his voice." (Ex 23:20-21a)

6 **Psalm 148:2   Full Angelic Chorus**
Praise him, all you his angels, / praise him, all you his hosts.

Angels are God's special gift to us. They help us in such a variety of ways here in this land of sojourn. Here is just one example.

Each time we offer Mass we become more and more aware of our own inadequacy in praising and thanking God, our gracious and generous Father. For this reason in the preface of the Mass we call upon all the choirs of heavenly hosts to help us in proclaiming the glory of God. We also join them in their unending hymn of praise.

With the angels let us sing: "Glory to God in high heaven, / peace on earth to those on whom / his favor rests." (Lk 2:14)

7 **Psalm 138:1   Super Power**
I will give thanks to you, O Lord, with all my heart, / in the presence of the angels I will sing your praise.

When we pause to reflect on the infinite goodness of God to us, we must conclude that we have no possible way of adequately expressing our thanks to him.

Our hearts may swell with profound sentiments of gratitude and appreciation, yet we feel helpless in manifesting our gratitude in words and deeds. What joy it gives us to realize that we can join our meager thanks to the whole choir of angels who offer an endless hymn of praise and glory to him for us.

The angels carry our prayer to the throne of God: "From the angel's hand the smoke of the incense went up before God, and with it the prayers of God's people." (Rev. 8:4)

Te Deum

O ne of the ancient hymns of praise and thanksgiving to God is called the *Te Deum* (We praise you, God). It was introduced about the fifth century.

The *Te Deum* is sometimes called a psalm of the Christian era since it resembles somewhat the ode format of the Old Testament psalms.

The *Te Deum* is used frequently in the Liturgy of the Hours. We are encouraged to use this hymn as a prayer of thanksgiving. It is often used in the church on the last day of the year to thank and praise our provident Father for all the blessings of the past year.

Since it bears a close relationship with the psalms, we have used it this week as a commentary with Psalm 148 to express our praise and gratitude to our benevolent God.

If you wish to pray the *Te Deum* in its entirety, you will find it at the end of this book.

1 Psalm 148:1   Enthroned in Majesty
Praise the Lord from the heavens, / praise him in the heights.

This powerful prayer of praise of the psalmist is incorporated into the church's liturgical hymn of praise, the *Te Deum.* "You are God: we praise you; / You are the Lord; we acclaim you; / You are the eternal Father; / All creation worships you."

Jesus taught us how to praise the Father: "I have given you glory on earth / by finishing the work you gave me to do." (Jn 17:4)

2 Psalm 148:2   The Powers of Heaven
Praise him, all you his angels / praise him, all you his hosts.

Again in the *Te Deum*, we continue to voice our praise of God united with all the choirs of angels in heaven. "To you all angels, all the powers of heaven, / Cherubim and Seraphim, sing in endless praise; / Holy, holy, holy, Lord God of power and might, / heaven and earth are full of your glory."

We join the angels in praising and glorifying God when we say: "In him everything in heaven and on earth was created, things visible and invisible, whether thrones or dominations, principalities or powers; all were created through him, and for him." (Col 1:16)

3 Psalm 148:3   Stars Shining With Joy
Praise him, sun and moon; / praise him, all you shining stars.

"The glorious company of apostles praise you. / The noble fellowship of prophets praise you. / The white-robed army of martyrs praise you."

The apostles, prophets, and martyrs, like "shining stars," praised God by accepting and fulfilling their mission in life. We are invited and urged to follow their example. Paul's directive will guide us: "Prove yourselves innocent and straightforward, children of God beyond reproach in the midst of a twisted and depraved generation—among whom you shine like the stars in the sky while holding fast to the word of life." (Phil 2:15-16a)

4 Psalm 148:5-6 Triple Praise
Let them praise the name of the Lord, / for he commanded and they were created; / He established them forever and ever; / he gave them a duty which shall not pass away.

"Throughout the world the holy Church acclaims you; / Father of majesty unbounded, / your true and only Son, worthy of all worship, / and the Holy Spirit, advocate and guide."

In his last discourse, Jesus gave us an insight into the work of the Holy Trinity. "When the Paraclete comes, / the Spirit of truth who comes from the Father— / and whom I myself will send from the Father— / he will bear witness on my behalf." (Jn 15:26)

5 Psalm 148:7 King of Glory
Praise the Lord from the earth, / you sea monsters and all depths.

"You, Christ, are the king of glory, / the eternal Son of the Father. / When you became man to set us free / you did not spurn the Virgin's womb."

Jesus became man not only to redeem us but to remain with us to teach us how to praise his Father. He took on our human nature with all its limitations so that he could live with us and within us. Jesus fulfilled what had been prophesied: "The virgin shall be with child / and give birth to a son, / and they shall call him Emmanuel." (Mt 1:23)

6 Psalm 148:13   Glorious Victory
Praise the name of the Lord, / for his name alone is exalted; / His majesty is above earth and heaven.

"You overcame the sting of death, / and opened the kingdom of heaven to all believers. / You are seated at God's right hand in glory, / We believe that you will come and be our judge."

By his passion, death and resurrection, Jesus opened the gates of his kingdom to all who believe. He is in his glory now, but his glory consists in continuing his redemptive work in us. For this reason we can rejoice triumphantly with St. Paul when he says: "Death is swallowed up in victory." "O death, where is your victory? O death, where is your sting?" (1 Cor 15:54b-55a)

7 Psalm 148:14b   His Chosen Family
Be this his praise from all the faithful ones, / from the children of Israel, the people close to him. / Alleluia.

"Come then, Lord, and help your people, / bought with the price of your own blood, / and bring us with your saints / to glory everlasting."

We are "the faithful ones." We are "the children of the new Israel." In our baptism we were not only buried with Christ but we will also rise gloriously with him.

St. Paul states it in these few words: "If we have been united with him through likeness to his death, so shall we be through a like resurrection." (Rom 6:5)

Part XI

Put Your Trust in God.

(Mk 11:22)

WEEK FORTY-ONE
Do We Really Trust?

We pray the psalms regularly and repeatedly in order to experience the power and presence, the loving care and concern, which the Lord has for each one of us.

Praying the psalms repeatedly transforms our hearts and minds. It helps us form deep and strong Christlike habits and patterns which influence our attitudes and actions.

One special habit which constantly needs augmenting is our trust and confidence in our loving Father and in his plans for us.

It is so easy for us to fear, doubt, or even mistrust the Lord when hardships and difficulties, when pains and suffering, descend upon us. Let us listen to what the inspired writer says to us this week about trust in God.

1 **Psalm 2:12   Trust in God**
Happy are all who take refuge in him!

Jesus is fully aware of everything which happens to us. He has already experienced the same joys and sorrows we encounter on our pilgrimage through life.

The risen Jesus is dwelling with us. He is the source of our strength and inspiration. He is the cause of our joy and happiness.

The more we trust him, the greater will be his response to us in any need. Jesus pleads with us: "Put your trust in God." (Mk 11:22)

201

2 Psalm 27:1   Trust Has No Fears
The Lord is my light and my salvation; / whom should I fear? The Lord is my life's refuge; / of whom should I be afraid?

Like the psalmist we need to ask ourselves often: Whom shall I fear, or of whom should I be afraid? When we pose these questions to ourselves, we begin to realize more deeply that the Lord has always protected and guided us. He has shielded us from harm on more occasions than we will ever know.

Moreover, he is our light guiding us on the road to salvation. As we recall the goodness of the Lord, our trust in him is greatly increased.

How well the sacred writer has reminded us: "If God is for us, who can be against us?" (Rom 8:31)

3 Psalm 27:4   Presence Strengthens Trust
To dwell in the house of the Lord / all the days of my life, / That I may gaze on the loveliness of the Lord / and contemplate his temple.

As we meditate on these words, we intensify our desire for a deeper, richer, more personal relationship with the Lord. Dwelling in the house of the Lord means abiding in his presence and being aware of his indwelling within us.

As we enter into the prayer of the heart, or the prayer of listening, we are gazing on the loveliness of the Lord. Such prayer has a powerful transforming effect upon us. It builds our confidence and trust in our gracious Father.

St. Paul put this thought in these words: "All of us, gazing on the Lord's glory with unveiled faces, are being transformed from glory to glory into his very image by the Lord who is the Spirit." (2 Cor 3:18)

4 Psalm 27:13-14   Faith Augments Trust

I believe that I shall see the bounty of the Lord / in the land of the living. / Wait for the Lord with courage; / be stouthearted, and wait for the Lord.

How necessary and how powerful are the words "I believe." Each time we make this act of faith in the goodness of the Lord, we are bolstering our confidence and trust.

Waiting for the Lord means resting in his presence, hoping, trusting, listening. This kind of prayer will increase our courage and make us more stouthearted in times of trial and tribulation.

With the father of the possessed boy, let us say to Jesus: "I do believe! Help my lack of trust!" (Mk 9:24)

5 Psalm 33:20-21   Trust Begets Joy

Our soul waits for the Lord, / who is our help and our shield. / For in him our hearts rejoice; / in his holy name we trust.

One of the finest expressions of love is our trust and confidence in the person we love. This is one of the greatest compliments we can pay to our loved one.

We need to hear ourselves verbalizing our trust in the Lord in order to form the habit pattern of trusting him always and in everything.

St. Paul says: "I rejoice because I trust you utterly." (2 Cor 7:16)

6 Psalm 4:6 Love Trusts
Offer just sacrifices, / and trust in the Lord.

In all the happenings of daily living, the Lord asks us to trust him. He has a special purpose for everything which comes our way.

Sacrifice is offering God the gift of ourselves. A heart filled with reverence and love, with confidence and trust, is a gift most pleasing to our benevolent Father.

St. Paul sums it up so masterfully: "There is no limit to love's forbearance, to its trust, its hope, its power to endure." (1 Cor 13:7)

7 Psalm 52:10 Safe Haven
But I, like a green olive tree in the house of God, / Trust in the kindness of God forever and ever.

In a game reserve animals and birds are protected and nourished. Such a sanctuary is a dependable and safe haven for them.

Metaphorically, the Lord is our refuge. When we abide in his presence, he protects and provides for us spiritually, physically, and psychologically, "in the house of God."

At times others may unintentionally or deliberately fail us, but we can always rely on the Lord for he is our faithful Father. St. Peter expressed his trust when he said: "Lord, to whom shall we go? You have the words of eternal life. We have come to believe; we are convinced that you are God's holy one." (Jn 6:68-69)

Fear Is Useless

Most of us live with a feeling of insecurity. Fear dominates our life, making it hard to trust completely.

Strange to say, it is even more difficult for us to trust God. We feel that others, who know our human limitations, will not expect too much from us, but we are not certain about God. He may ask more than we want to give.

May the suggested verses of the psalms for this week greatly increase and strengthen our trust.

1 Psalm 37:3-5   No Better Security

Trust in the Lord and do good, / that you may dwell in the land and enjoy security. / Take delight in the Lord, / and he will grant you your heart's requests. / Commit to the Lord your way; / trust in him, and he will act.

When we keep our way of life in tune with the will of the Lord, we will enjoy a peace and security which the world cannot give. As we strive to commit our life to him, "he will act" by bestowing every gift and blessing we need on our journey heavenward. What more could we ask?

The sacred writer's urging gives us even more hope: "Let us hold unswervingly to our profession which gives us hope, for he who made the promise deserves our trust." (Heb 10:23)

2 Psalm 40:4   Trust Begets Joy

He put a new song into my mouth, / a hymn to our God. / Many shall look on in awe / and trust in the Lord.

Our confidence and trust in the Lord will increase the joy and happiness in our own lives. When we pause to reflect on the Lord's loving care and concern for us, our hearts will become more joyous and it will "put a new song into our mouth."

Our rejoicing in the Lord is contagious. It will encourage others to place more trust and confidence in him. It will bring greater peace and joy in their lives also.

Isaiah says: "Trust in the Lord forever! / For the Lord is an eternal Rock." (Is 26:4)

3 Psalm 49:7-8   False Security

They trust in their wealth; / the abundance of their riches is their boast. / Yet in no way can a man redeem himself, / or pay his own ransom to God.

In our age we have witnessed near miraculous achievements in our technological discoveries. These advances have made us a proud, self-sufficient people even to the extent of questioning our dependence upon God.

To counteract such a tendency we need only recall that the Creator of the universe has provided all these secrets which we are just beginning to unlock.

How valid is the truth advanced by the psalmist many centuries ago: "Yet in no way can a man redeem himself, / or pay his own ransom to God."

4 Psalm 56:4-5   No Room for Fear

O Most High, when I begin to fear / in you will I trust. / In God, in whose promise I glory, / in God I trust without fear; / what can flesh do against me?

Trust is one of the many fruits of love. When we love a person we will trust that person. When we love God by trying to live according to his will, we have no reason to fear.

Furthermore, our trust in the Lord will eliminate the fear of being criticized, rejected, or persecuted by others.

According to St. John, our trust is in proportion to our love. He writes: "Love has no room for fear; / rather, perfect love casts out all fear." (1 Jn 4:18a)

5 Psalm 62:9   Firm Foundation

Trust in him at all times, O my people! / Pour out your hearts before him; / God is our refuge!

These inspired words encourage us to place implicit trust in God at all times. Trust in God is a quiet, peaceful, tranquil assurance that God loves us so much that he cares for us at every moment of the day. It is not a frenzied crying out for immediate help in a desperate moment. In fact, real trust does not experience these moments.

Trust is the fruit of love. When we love God as our kind Father, we can pour out our hearts before him, knowing that he cares.

Jesus emphasizes the importance of trust: "Trust me when I tell you that whoever does not accept the kingdom of God as a child will not enter into it." (Lk 18:17)

208 / Rejoice In Me

6 Psalm 71:5-6 Blessing in Disguise
For you are my hope, O Lord; / my trust, O God, from my youth. / On you I depend from birth; / from my mother's womb you are my strength; / constant has been my hope in you.

A brief review of our life will reveal how faithful God has been to us from the time of our first breath until this very heartbeat. Such a reflection will stimulate our hope and strengthen our trust in him.

If we have had an apparently tragic or traumatic experience in the past, our trust in the Lord may have wavered temporarily. However, looking upon that experience in retrospect may help us to understand that it was a blessing in disguise.

Sirach encourages us not to lose hope: "Trust God and he will help you; / make straight your ways and hope in him." (Sir 2:6)

7 Psalm 84:13 Happiness Is Trust
O Lord of hosts, / happy the men who trust in you!

Most of us have a rather low self-image. We are insecure because of this low profile. The most effective way for us to build a healthy self-image is to know that God accepts and loves us just as we are.

To be convinced that God loves us, we must trust him. This trust will make us a happy person.

Sirach's words will help us trust in the Lord and enjoy genuine happiness. "Happy the soul that fears the Lord! / In whom does he trust, and who is his support? / The eyes of the Lord are upon those who love him; / he is their mighty shield and strong support." (Sir 34:15f)

What Is Needed Is Trust

Genuine trust springs from the theological virtues of faith, hope, and love.

If we have faith, trust will blossom forth.

If we have hope, trust will flourish.

If we have love, trust will endure.

Jesus always pleaded for a firm trust in him and in the teachings he set forth. He gave us countless reasons for a full-fledged trust in him.

May our prayer of listening this week strengthen our trust in him and make it dynamic and vigorous.

1 Psalm 25:1-2 Fervent Prayer

To you I lift up my soul, / O Lord, my God. / In you I trust; / let me not be put to shame.

This is a fervent prayer for a greater trust and confidence in our almighty Father. We want to trust him implicitly. We do not want to doubt him. However, because of our human short-sightedness, we do have fears and misgivings at times.

The Father understands our humanness and patiently waits for us to accept his love with its companions of trust and confidence. The words of Wisdom will increase our trust: "Those who trust in him shall understand truth, / and the faithful shall abide with him in love: / Because grace and mercy are with his holy ones, / and his care is with his elect." (Wis 3:9)

2 Psalm 52:9 Trust Misplaced
"This is the man who made not / God the source of his strength, / But put his trust in his great wealth, / and his strength in harmful plots."

Jesus illustrated this truth in the parable of the rich man who was blessed with an abundant harvest. He rebuilt his grain bins to store his harvest. He was not concerned about thanking God for his good fortune, nor was he willing to share with those less fortunate. He was thinking only of himself, his ease and comfort.

He said to himself: " 'Relax, eat heartily, drink well. Enjoy yourself.' But God said to him: 'You fool! This very night your life shall be required of you. To whom will all this piled-up wealth of yours go?'" Jesus drew this moral: "That is the way it works with the man who grows rich for himself instead of growing rich in the sight of God." (Lk 12:16f)

3 Psalm 93:5 Paving the Way
Your decrees are worthy of trust indeed: / holiness befits your house, / O Lord, for length of days.

The Father has given us decrees, directives, and regulations to guide us on our journey home to heaven. These may challenge us at times. They may even run counter to our own desires and ambitions. Yet they "are worthy of trust indeed" because they give us an opportunity to give our will as a love-offering to the Father.

In this, Jesus showed us the way. He was most solicitous to do exactly what the Father asked of him because he loved his Father with an infinite love.

If we fail we can trust that we will be forgiven: "But if we acknowledge our sins / he who is just can be trusted / to forgive our sins / and cleanse us from every wrong." (1 Jn 1:9)

4 Psalm 115:11   Faithful Father
Those who fear the Lord trust in the Lord; / he is their help and their shield.

God is our gracious Abba. He wants to be a generous and loving Father to us. In his word he repeatedly tells us: "I will be their God and they shall be my people." He continues: "I will welcome you and be a father to you and you will be my sons and daughters" (2 Cor 6:16ff).

What greater reason could he give us to win our trust in him? Let us heed the advice of the sacred writer: "So let us confidently approach the throne of grace to receive mercy and favor and to find help in time of need." (Heb 4:16)

5 Psalm 119:66   Teach by Witnessing
Teach me wisdom and knowledge, / for in your commands I trust.

We teach a spiritual truth not by a rational presentation but by witnessing to it in our own lives. We may speak eloquently of the necessity of having a deep and firm trust in God, but it will not be convincing unless our own life reflects an unwavering trust and confidence in our gracious Father.

Practicing what we preach may be a trite old adage, but its truth is verifiable nonetheless.

The royal official gave us a compelling example by believing Jesus when he said: "'Your son will live!' The man put his trust in the word Jesus spoke to him, and started for home." (Jn 4:50f)

6 Psalm 130:5   Powerful Word
I trust in the Lord; / my soul trusts in his word.

Love begets trust. Our love of God generates within us a firm trust and a greater confidence in our Father. We trust "in his word" by which he reveals to us how much he loves us. In his word he tells us why he does so much for us: "Because you are precious in my eyes / and glorious, and because I love you. . . ." (Is 43:4)

Jesus confirms his own love for us: "As the Father has loved me, / so I have loved you. / Live on in my love." (Jn 15:9)

St. Paul's words are a classic: "There is no limit to love's forbearance, to its trust, its hope, its power to endure." (1 Cor 13:7)

7 Psalm 146:3-4   Be Mindful of the Lord
Put not your trust in princes, / in man, in whom there is no salvation. / When his spirit departs he returns to his earth; / on that day his plans perish.

We readily seek the advice and guidance of others. We may even regard their counsel and opinions as infallible. At other times we may depend solely on our own judgment.

God does want us to use our own intelligence and also to consult others, but he also wants us to listen to his inspirations and guidance, to his gift of discernment, especially in weighty matters. The Lord wants us to make our decision in the light of eternity. The inspired proverb admonishes us: "Trust in the Lord with all your heart, / on your own intelligence rely not; / In all your ways be mindful of him, / and he will make straight your paths." (Prv 3:5-6)

WEEK FORTY-FOUR

Sing Gratefully

St. Paul is a model pastor who is always advising, exhorting, and encouraging his flock. His directives are usually short and to the point. Here is one of his gems: "Sing gratefully to God from your hearts in psalms, hymns and inspired songs." (Col 3:16c)

The psalms are an ideal way for us to express our gratitude and praise to our loving Father. The Hebrew word for psalms (*tehillim*) means poems of praise composed to be sung.

The psalms draw us apart from the myriad mundane distractions of our workaday life into contemplative communication with God.

As you pray the psalms this week, let your heart sing!

1 Psalm 149:1 Community Crescendo
Sing to the Lord a new song / of praise in the assembly of the faithful.

This is an invitation to praise God with a new song. The song itself may not be new, but our sincerity and exuberance will be more intense as we contemplate God's extraordinary goodness.

Likewise the joy and praise in our hearts will swell into a mighty crescendo when we join with the liturgical assembly in praising and thanking the Lord. Such a celebration of praise and thanksgiving will strengthen the faith and appreciation of the whole community.

May the words of St. John be our prayer too: "We praise you, the Lord God Almighty, / who is and who was. / You have assumed your great power, / you have begun your reign." (Rev. 11:17)

213

2 Psalm 149:3   Postures of Praise
Let them praise his name in the festive dance, / let them sing praise to him with timbrel and harp.

A festive dance may seem a little unusual to us. Nevertheless, body language is an important method of communication. It manifests our interior dispositions. Miriam and all the women danced with joy when the Israelites crossed the Red Sea safely. David danced before the Ark of God when it was brought to the royal city.

Extended arms, folded hands, genuflections, and prostrations all reveal the prayerful attitude of our heart. To be sincere we must avoid mechanical gestures. Our posture must arise from a deep personal awareness of God's all-encompassing love.

St. Paul is speaking to us when he writes: "It is my wish, then, that in every place the men shall offer prayers with blameless hands held aloft, and be free from anger and dissension." (1 Tm 2:8)

3 Psalm 149:4   Worthy of Praise
For the Lord loves his people, / and he adorns the lowly with victory.

What an extraordinary statement! Despite all our infidelities and backsliding, the Lord loves us. We are his people.

The Lord looks deep into our heart. He knows our intentions. He realizes that we want to serve him perfectly, but he also knows our brokenness and our weaknesses. He loves us just as we are. The reason for our praise: "He adorns the lowly with victory."

How comforting are the words of Jesus: "The healthy do not need a doctor; sick people do. I have not come to invite the self-righteous to a change of heart, but sinners." (Lk 5:31-32)

4 Psalm 149:5-6   Assembly of Praise
Let the faithful exult in glory; / let them sing for joy upon their couches; / let the high praises of God be in their throats.

Our liturgical celebrations bring us together to raise a paean of praise to our heavenly Father. As we gather to offer Mass together, our praise takes on an even greater dimension because Jesus, our eternal high priest, accepts our praise, unites it with his own, and presents it to the Father in our name. Thus we are really offering "high praises to God."

The first Christians give us an encouraging example: "With exultant and sincere hearts they took their meals in common, praising God and winning the approval of all the people." (Acts 2:46b-47a)

5 Psalm 135:1-3   Name to be Praised
Praise the name of the Lord; / praise, you servants of the Lord / Who stand in the house of the Lord, / in the courts of the house of our God. / Praise the Lord, for the Lord is good; / sing praise to his name, which we love.

We are a privileged people. We enjoy the gift of faith. By our adoption as sons and daughters of the Father, we do "stand in the house of the Lord, in the courts of the house of our God."

We belong to the household of God. We are members of his family. Indeed, the Lord is good. How much we should praise his name. This realization should elicit hymns of joyous praise for this unique privilege.

St. John reminds us of this privilege: "Dearly beloved, we are God's children now; / what we shall later be has not yet come to light. / We know that when it comes to light / we shall be like him. . . ." (1 Jn 3:2)

6 **Psalm 33:1-2   Praise from Loving Hearts**
Exult, you just, in the Lord; / praise from the upright is fitting. / Give thanks to the Lord on the harp; / with the ten-stringed lyre chant his praises.

The "just and the upright" upon whom the poet calls are people like ourselves who love the Lord and are striving to live according to his will. Our prime prerogative and privilege is to praise God for himself and for all his divine attributes.

Praise is prayer in its highest form because God alone is the focus of our prayer. Our first duty is to recognize God our Father as Lord and Master of both the material and the spiritual worlds.

As a spiritual father, St. Paul advises us: "Sing praise to the Lord with all your hearts." (Eph 5:19b)

7 **Psalm 33:3-5   Shouts of Gladness**
Sing to him a new song; / pluck the strings skillfully, with shouts of gladness. / For upright is the word of the Lord, / and all his works are trustworthy. / He loves justice and right; / of the kindness of the Lord the earth is full.

Singing is an expression of joy. When we're happy and cheerful, our hearts naturally burst into song.

As we contemplate the kindness of the Lord of which the earth is full, or pause to recall his trustworthiness throughout the ages, our hearts will rejoice and songs of joy will invariably come from our lips. This is our invitation: "Praise our God, all you his servants, / the small and the great, who revere him!" (Rev 19:5)

Part XII

Come to Him, a Living Stone.

(1 Pt 2:4)

Solid as a Rock

It is impossible for us to grasp the immensity and the majesty of God. Our human limitations allow us only little glimpses now and then of his beauty and perfection.

In striving to comprehend something about God, the ancient Hebrews coined a proper name from one of the many attributes of God. Rock soon became one of God's divine titles.

The title Rock speaks to us of security, safety, protection, trustworthiness, fidelity—in a word, salvation.

Let us praise and thank the Rock of our Salvation!

1 Psalm 95:1-2   Rock of Joy

Come, let us sing joyfully to the Lord; / let us acclaim the Rock of our salvation. / Let us greet him with thanksgiving; / let us joyfully sing psalms to him.

God is the Rock of our salvation because he created us and destined us for a life of perfect happiness with him in heaven. Even though his ways may seem mysterious at times, they are all designed to lead us to our eternal goal.

Realizing that God is always faithful to his promises, songs of joy and thanksgiving arise in our hearts as we "sing joyfully to the Lord." The author of Hebrews gives us some sage advice: "Encourage one another daily while it is still 'today,' so that no one grows hardened by the deceit of sin." (Heb 3:13)

2 **Psalm 18:2-3 Loving Rock**
I love you, O Lord, my strength, / O Lord, my rock, my fortress, my deliverer. / My God, my rock of refuge, / my shield, the horn of my salvation, my stronghold!

The psalmist exhausts his vocabulary trying to relate all that God is to him.

When we realize the power and the love in God's protecting, encouraging, and reassuring love, we can say also with the poet: "I love you, O Lord, my strength."

Perhaps St. Thomas's brief summary could be our constant prayer: "My Lord and my God!" (Jn 20:28)

3 **Psalm 89:27 Father Rock**
"He shall say of me, 'You are my father, / my God, the rock, my savior.'"

According to God's plan, an ideal father of a family should be the epitome of everything good. He teaches and guides, he provides and protects his chidren. Above all, he loves them.

While a natural father may not be able to fulfill his role perfectly because of human limitations, he does nevertheless portray the role of our heavenly Father who is all things to us—God, Rock, Savior.

How briefly but how adequately the Spirit tells us: "I will be his God and he shall be my son." (Rev 21:7)

4 Psalm 144:1-2 Resilient Rock
Blessed be the Lord, my rock . . . / My refuge and my fortress, / my stronghold, my deliverer.

When Jesus became man he accepted all our human limitations. He shared our struggles. In doing so, he proved that God's strength manifests itself most clearly in weakness. Jesus' weakness wrought our salvation.

When we acknowledge our weakness, God becomes our Rock, our strength, and above all the source of our peace, happiness, and joy.

Jesus affirms this truth when he said: "I tell you all this / that in me you may find peace. / You will suffer in the world. / But take courage! / I have overcome the world." (Jn 16:33)

5 Psalm 75:6 Rock of Pride
Lift not up your horns against the Most High; / speak not haughtily against the Rock.

Our pride may prompt us to question God's ways in our life. At times we may even become angry with God because certain events did not happen as we had planned. Our pride may blind us so that we cannot understand why certain crosses and disappointments come our way.

We easily forget that God said: "For my thoughts are not your thoughts, nor are your ways my ways" (Is 55:8). We are not always aware that God may humble us so that he can exalt us.

Our Blessed Mother reminds us: "He has shown might with his arm; / he has confused the proud in their inmost thoughts. / He has deposed the mighty from their thrones / and raised the lowly to high places." (Lk 1:51-52)

6 **Psalm 18:32-33 Secure Rock**
For who is God except the Lord? / Who is a rock, save our God? / The God who girded me with strength / and kept my way unerring.

A rock conjures up in our minds a sense of security. We immediately think of a firm foundation, a solid shelter, a safe harbor.

Jesus is our Rock, the cornerstone on which our spiritual growth and maturation is built. He alone gives us the strength to keep our way unerring.

He himself said: "Anyone who hears my words and puts them into practice is like the wise man who built his house on rock. When the rainy season set in, the torrents came and the winds blew and buffeted his house. It did not collapse; it had been solidly set on rock." (Mt 7:24-25)

7 **Psalm 92:15-16 Foundation Rock**
They shall bear fruit even in old age; / vigorous and sturdy shall they be, / Declaring how just is the Lord, / my Rock, in whom there is no wrong.

God's plan for us extends to every moment of our life and includes even the smallest detail. He is truly the rock foundation of our lives. We honor and serve him by all that we are, as well as by what we do and say. This is our mission in life.

Our attitudes and also our actions "declare how just is the Lord," thus paving the way for others to recognize him as the Rock in their lives.

St. Paul tells us how much we need the Lord: "In him who is the source of my strength I have the strength for everything." (Phil 4:13)

Jesus, the Rock

Rock is a symbol of sterility and dryness, yet by his almighty power God provided water in abundance from a waterless rock for the Israelites in a barren desert.

This divine manifestation of God's loving care and concern paved the way for the eschatological wonders of the "living waters" —the divine life— flowing from the spiritual Rock who is Christ Jesus.

May the following reflections bring us to a deeper appreciation of the wonders of God's love for us!

1 Psalm 28:1   Benevolent Rock

To you, O Lord, I call; / O my Rock, be not deaf to me, / Lest, if you heed me not, / I become one of those going down into the pit.

Our heavenly Father wants to be an indulgent Abba to us. He hears our prayer and will respond to all our needs if we approach him with humility, sincerity, and confidence.

Listen to his divine promise: "When you call me, when you go to pray to me, I will listen to you. When you look for me, you will find me. Yes, when you seek me with all your heart, you will find me with you." (Jer 29:12-14a)

2 Psalm 61:3-4a Rock of Safety
From the earth's end I call to you / as my heart grows faint. / You will set me high upon a rock; / you will give me rest, / for you are my refuge.

The poet paints an authentic picture of our journey through life. The "earth's end" speaks of our own helplessness, while our many weaknesses cause our "heart to grow faint."

God's response is to set us "high upon a rock" which manifests the loving care and concern of the Lord who rescues us in our need, especially our spiritual need.

We have this reassurance from St. Paul: "God keeps his promise. He will not let you be tested beyond your strength. Along with the test he will give you a way out of it so that you may be able to endure it." (1 Cor 10:13)

3 Psalm 78:15 Miraculous Rock
He cleft the rocks in the desert / and gave them water in copious floods. / He made streams flow from the crag / and brought the waters forth in rivers.

Water is absolutely essential for the preservation of life. In the desert, God stripped the Israelites of everything so that they could learn total dependence upon him. He supplied them with water from a waterless rock. Jesus is the living water in our lives. The living water which he shares with us is his own divine life as a preparation for the fullness of divine life in heaven. Jesus invites us to come to him for this living water: "If anyone thirsts, let him come to me; / let him drink who believes in me.... From within him rivers of living water shall flow." (Jn 7:37b-38)

4 Psalm 27:5   High on a Rock
For he will hide me in his abode / in the day of trouble; / He will conceal me in the shelter of his tent, / he will set me high upon a rock.

These words urge us to place unbounded confidence and trust in God our Father. In this prayer the psalmist assures us that the Lord will rescue us when we are threatened. He will come to our aid any time we need him.

The metaphor "high upon a rock" gives us an added reason for confidence and trust. We can be certain that God stands by us at all times. As the sacred writer tells us: "This is God's dwelling among men. He shall dwell with them and they shall be his people and he shall be their God who is always with them." (Rev 21:3b)

5 Psalm 105:41   Rock of Living Water
He cleft the rock, and the water gushed forth; / it flowed through the dry lands like a stream.

This miraculous supply of water from a rock in a barren desert has a deep eschatological meaning.

By his redemption, Jesus is the source of living water which nourishes and strengthens us as we journey through this land of exile. His divine power in giving the Israelites the gushing water is the same power filling us with his divine life.

St. Paul recalls for us this event in these words: "All drank the same spiritual drink (they drank from the spiritual rock that was following them, and the rock was Christ)." (1 Cor 10:4)

6 Psalm 114:7-8 Provident Rock
Before the face of the Lord, tremble, O earth, / before the face of the God of Jacob, / Who turned the rock into pools of water, / the flint into flowing springs.

Flint rock is the most unlikely source of water in a desert. Yet by God's might and power, rock became pools of fresh water to save his people.

That same divine power and might watches over us and provides for all our needs both physical and spiritual. All the Lord asks of us is to believe and trust in him. Jesus assures us as he did Martha: "Did I not assure you that if you believed you would see the glory of God displayed?" (Jn 11:40)

7 Psalm 19:15 Rock of Salvation
Let the words of my mouth and the thought of my heart / find favor before you, / O Lord, my rock and my redeemer.

This is a humble prayer that we may have the proper disposition of mind and heart when we turn to the Lord for help. When we recognize our own inability and our dependence upon God, then he will respond most graciously and generously to our prayer.

With the psalmist let us ask that our words and our thoughts may always be in tune with the mind and heart of the Lord.

Listen to what the Lord says: "I, the Lord, alone probe the mind / and test the heart, / To reward everyone according to his ways, / according to the merit of his deeds." (Jer 17:10)

God's Saving Love

God created us for himself. He wants to share his divine life with us in the joyous bliss of perfect love in heaven.

Even as Adam and Eve refused God's love when they sinned, God promised them a Redeemer who would restore that fragmented relationship between himself and sinful mankind.

He announced through the prophet: "I take no pleasure in the death of a wicked man, but rather in the wicked man's conversion" (Ez 33:11).

In brief, God wants our salvation more than we could want it ourselves. May his inspired word find a home in our heart. It will cause us much joy.

1 Psalm 119:174-175 Ardent Longing
I long for your salvation, O Lord, / and your law is my delight. / Let my soul live to praise you, / and may your ordinances help me.

There is within everyone of us a longing, a desire, a void which can be filled only by God. St. Augustine said it this way: "Our hearts are restless until they rest in Thee."

This longing can be completely satisfied only in heaven. In his goodness the Lord has given us his law and ordinances to guide us heavenward. Realizing this we can say with the sacred writer: "Your law is my delight and your ordinances help me." Jesus invites us in these words: "Let him who is thirsty come forward; let all who desire it accept the gift of life-giving water." (Rev 22:17b)

2 Psalm 3:8a, 9   No Greater Gift
Rise up, O Lord! / Save me, my God! / Salvation is the Lord's! / Upon your people be your blessing.

God is pleased when we come to him with childlike confidence and humility to place our needs before him and beg his help. Our final goal is our eternal salvation. It is God's gift to us if we implore him and prepare ourselves to receive it. As we plead for this most gracious gift, our hearts are already being transformed to receive it.

Salvation is the greatest of all gifts because it is the gift of God himself as he shares his divine life with us.

Jesus encouraged us to pray in this way: "Ask, and you will receive. Seek, and you will find. Knock, and it will be opened to you. For the one who asks, receives. The one who seeks, finds. The one who knocks, enters." (Mt 7:7-8)

3 Psalm 91:15-16   Call upon the Lord
He shall call upon me, and I will answer him; / I will be with him in distress; / I will deliver him and glorify him; / with length of days I will gratify him / and will show him my salvation.

Through the psalmist the Lord promised us that he would be with us in all distress and difficulties. Furthermore, he would bless us and all our endeavors.

There are only two conditions required: we must call upon him and also be pliable in his hands.

Jesus reiterated the promise of the Father: "Anyone who loves me / will be true to my word, / and my Father will love him; / we will come to him / and make our dwelling place with him." (Jn 14:23)

4 Psalm 119:154-155   Afraid to Love
Plead my cause, and redeem me; / for the sake of your promise give me life. / Far from sinners is salvation, / because they seek not your statutes.

A person who sins is refusing to accept the love which our Father wishes to pour out upon him or her. Sin says no to love.

Sin is tragic because it is the only thing which can prevent us from reaching our eternal happiness. Unfortunately, sin not only harms the sinner but also impedes the Lord's divine life and love being poured out upon the whole body of Christ.

On the other hand, the Lord's statutes are directives enabling us to receive God's love. They are also the avenues leading us to our eternal salvation.

Listen to the tenderness in Jesus' words as he says: " 'It is mercy I desire and not sacrifice.' I have come to call, not the self-righteous, but sinners." (Mt 9:13)

5 Psalm 38:22-23   Never Forsaken
Forsake me not, O Lord; / my God, be not far from me! / Make haste to help me, / O Lord, my salvation!

Salvation is a precious gift from God. However, the Lord never imposes his gifts upon us. He patiently waits for us to be receptive to his transforming power and love.

An essential condition in preparing ourselves for salvation is our attitude of mind and heart. We must acknowledge our sinfulness, be humbly contrite, and permit the Lord to mold and transform us. Listen to the psalmist's fervent and humble prayer for the Lord's help. "God has said, 'I will never desert you, nor will I forsake you.' " (Heb 13:5)

6 Psalm 85:8   Unfailing Fidelity

Show us, O Lord, your kindness, / and grant us your salvation.

In scriptural parlance, God's kindness is a sort of umbrella which covers so many of his divine attributes. It means particularly his fidelity. God promised us salvation. He sent his Son, Jesus, into the world to redeem us. Jesus also taught us the way to spiritual growth and left us his own example as a model for our lifestyle.

This sublime truth is the cause of our joy. Continue to ask the Lord for the gift of salvation.

In his hymn of praise, Zechariah sang: "All this is the work of the kindness of our God; / he, the Dayspring, shall visit us in his mercy / To shine on those who sit in darkness and in the shadow of death, / to guide our feet into the way of peace." (Lk 1:78-79)

7 Psalm 96:1-2   Fountain of Salvation

Sing to the Lord a new song; / sing to the Lord, all you lands. / Sing to the Lord, bless his name; / announce his salvation, day after day.

What greater joy could come to us than knowing that the Lord loves us so much that he has saved us. He wants us with him for all eternity.

Our joy-filled hearts want to burst forth with a new song for all people to hear as we daily announce his salvation.

Isaiah prepared us for this happy task: "With joy you will draw water / at the fountain of salvation, and say on that day: / Give thanks to the Lord, acclaim his name; / among the nations make known his deeds, / proclaim how exalted is his name." (Is 12:3-4)

Love Wrought Our Salvation

In one brief statement St. John capsulizes the whole mystery of our salvation from the incarnation to the passion and death and climaxing in the resurrection of Jesus. John writes:

> "Yes, God so loved the world, / that he gave his only Son, / that whoever believes in him may not die / but may have eternal life." (Jn 3:16)

We find great comfort in St. Paul's teaching: "God is rich in mercy; because of his great love for us he brought us to life with Christ when we were dead in sin. By this favor you were saved" (Eph 2:4-5). Pondering these words makes us want to shout with joy, praise, and thanksgiving to our merciful Father.

1 Psalm 26:11-12 Level Ground

But I walk in integrity; / redeem me, and have pity on me. / My foot stands on level ground; / in the assemblies I will bless the Lord.

The psalmist's affirmation gives us inspiration and motivation. He recognizes that God has pity on us and has redeemed us. Furthermore, Jesus has given us a way of life to follow. He taught us by his own lifestyle.

The psalmist is striving to live this way of life. Therefore, he can say: "I walk in integrity." He inspires us to stand on this "level ground" and continue to bless the Lord in everything we do.

How aptly St. Peter's words apply: "When God raised up his servant, he sent him to you first to bless you by turning you from your evil ways." (Acts 3:26)

2 Psalm 66:4   Grand Chorus
*Let all on earth worship and sing praise to you, /
sing praise to your name!*

The poet pleads for all the earth to sing the
praises of God because he has delivered us from
our sinfulness and is leading us into eternal glory.
If all people would unite their hearts and voices in
praise of God, a tremendous paean of praise would
rise heavenward.

Even though we have no visible community
joining us, our praise, nonetheless, is united with
that grand chorus of praise of all our brothers and
sisters on earth as well as the whole host of heaven.

In speaking of the Eucharist, St. Paul reminds
us: "Is not the bread we break a sharing in the body
of Christ? Because the loaf of bread is one, we,
many though we are, are one body, for we all
partake of the one loaf." (1 Cor 10:16-17)

3 Psalm 77:14-15   Review of Life
*O God, your way is holy; / what great god is there
like our God? / You are the God who works wonders; /
among the peoples you have made known your power.*

The history of salvation is one continuous series
of God's great works and wonders among his
people. His mighty and miraculous works reveal
not only his divine power but also his loving
concern for every individual person.

If we review our own life year by year, we will
discover with awe and gratitude the tremendous
deeds he has performed at every step of our
pilgrimage. Surely he is "the God who works
wonders." Such a recalling fills us with joyful
praise and thanksgiving.

What greater assurance can we have than the
Lord's words: "My love shall never leave you / nor
my covenant of peace be shaken . . ." (Is 54:10b)

4 Psalm 97:12 Touched with Glory
Be glad in the Lord, you just, / and give thanks to his holy name.

Here we are advised to "be glad in the Lord." Love, peace, joy are the hallmark of a just person. These are special gifts of the Holy Spirit dwelling within us. Gladness and joy will be ours as we strive to walk in the way of the Lord.

The main source of our joy is the revelation which Jesus gave us when he told us of the boundless, enduring love of the Father for us. Jesus added a special bonus when he assured us that his love for us is equally great. For this great love let us "give thanks to his holy name."

St. Peter gives us cause to rejoice: "Although you have never seen him, you love him, and without seeing you now believe in him, and rejoice with inexpressible joy touched with glory because you are achieving faith's goal, your salvation." (1 Pt 1:8-9)

5 Psalm 103:22 Infinite Compassion
Bless the Lord, all his works, / everywhere in his domain. / Bless the Lord, O my soul!

We are called upon to join the heavenly spirits and all creation in its hymn of grateful praise to the Lord. We bless the Lord for his continuous compassion for us sinners. He heals our weaknesses, forgives our failures, and saves us from eternal doom. He does this so that we may be with him in heaven to praise and glorify him forever. Let today be a day of thanksgiving and praise.

With Zechariah let us sing his praises: "All this is the work of the kindness of our God; / he, the Dayspring, shall visit us in his mercy." (Lk 1:78)

6 **Psalm 104:35 Happy Day**
May sinners cease from the earth / and may the wicked be no more. Bless the Lord, O my soul! Alleluia.

In these words we are really praying for ourselves. We are painfully aware of our sinfulness and we pray that we might be freed from our propensity to sin.

St. Paul lamented that in spite of his good intention and his desire to live a sinless life, he fell again and again. Listen to his own words: "What happens is that I do, not the good I will to do, but the evil I do not intend" (Rom 7:19). His words reflect our own condition. In desperation Paul cries out: "What a wretched man I am! Who can free me from this body under the power of death?" (Rom 7:24). Then he remembers and also reminds us that Jesus alone is our Savior and Redeemer. We join him as he exclaims: "All praise to God, through Jesus Christ our Lord!" (Rom 7:25)

7 **Psalm 106:47 No Greater Gift**
Save us, O Lord, our God, / and gather us from among the nations, / That we may give thanks to your holy name / and glory in praising you.

Salvation is God's gift to us. As St. Paul reminds us, salvation is not our own doing, nor is it a reward for anything we have accomplished.

Giving "thanks to his holy name and glory in praising him" is an ideal method of preparing for this tremendous gift.

St. Paul is quite eloquent when he speaks about our redemption: "He likewise predestined us through Christ Jesus to be his adopted sons— such was his will and pleasure—that all might praise the glorious favor he has bestowed on us in his beloved." (Eph 1:5-6)

Part XIII

Tidings of Great Joy

(Lk 2:10)

Joy of Salvation

There is no greater blessing than a deep, vibrant, interior joy which comes to us from the realization that we are saved. God loves us so much that he wants us united with him in the trinitarian community of perfect love.

Salvation is a gift from our benevolent Father. St. Paul tells us: "It is owing to his favor that salvation is yours through faith. This is not your own doing, it is God's gift" (Eph 2:8).

Accepting this truth in faith will enable us to be open and receptive to his gift. Our faith will enable us also to prepare ourselves to receive such a tremendous gift. Each day let us thank God for his saving love.

1 Psalm 68:20-21 Saving Love
Blessed day by day be the Lord, / who bears our burdens; God who is our salvation. / God is a saving God for us; / the Lord, my Lord, controls the passageways of death.

As Savior, Jesus accepted "the burdens" of our sinfulness and by his redemption reestablished our relationship with the Father.

He is our saving God. By his redemptive love, he conquered death and thus "controls the passageways of death," making death the doorway into our eternal union with him in perfect love. How gracious is the promise of Jesus: "I solemnly assure you, / the man who hears my word / and has faith in him who sent me / possesses eternal life. / He does not come under condemnation, / but has passed from death to life." (Jn 5:24)

2 Psalm 106:4-5   Eternal Glory

Remember me, O Lord, as you favor your people; / visit me with your saving help, / That I may see the prosperity of your chosen ones, / rejoice in the joy of your people, / and glory with your inheritance.

If we strive to live the way of life Jesus outlined for us, particularly in the Beatitudes, we will come into our inheritance, which is heaven. Jesus promised this in so many different words in the Beatitudes: inherit the land; the reign of God; shall see God; shall be called sons and daughters of God.

Our hearts are jubilant because Jesus not only promised us our inheritance but he solemnly prayed for it. "Father, / all those you gave me / I would have in my company / where I am, / to see this glory of mine / which is your gift to me. . . ."(Jn 17:24)

3 Psalm 118:24-25   Happiest of Days

This is the day the Lord has made; / let us be glad and rejoice in it. / O Lord, grant salvation! / O Lord, grant prosperity!

Each new day is another gift from our most gracious Father. It is another chapter in our lives. It is one more step forward on our journey heavenward.

Every day is a golden opportunity for us to offer to God the gift of ourselves along with everything we do, think, and say. Each day he asks us to be receptive to and cooperative with his redemptive love, to permit him to forgive and redeem us.

We have a splendid example in the criminal on the cross. Because he was contrite and receptive, Jesus could say to him: "I assure you: this day you will be with me in paradise." (Lk 23:43)

4 Psalm 13:6 Life Eternal

Let my heart rejoice in your salvation; / let me sing of the Lord, "He has been good to me."

Many times in life we have a sense of frustration. We are busily engaged in activity which bears little or no fruit. We see the futility of so many things we do. Life seems so fleeting and ephemeral.

The Lord may permit us to experience these feelings in order to impress upon us that we have no lasting home here on earth.

What joy is ours when we hear the Lord saying to us: "I am indeed going to prepare a place for you, / and then I shall come back to take you with me, / that where I am you also may be." (Jn 14:3)

5 Psalm 71:23-24 No Greater Love

My lips shall shout for joy / as I sing your praises; / My soul also, which you have redeemed, / and my tongue day by day shall discourse on your justice.

Our lips want to shout for joy because our hearts are filled with inexpressible joy in knowing that eternal salvation is ours. Why can we be so certain that we are saved?

Scripture is filled with reassurances of our salvation. God so loved us that he gave us the greatest of all gifts—his only Son Jesus as our Redeemer. Jesus loved us so much that he willingly laid down his life for our redemption. He solemnly promised us that we would rise and be happy with him for all eternity. Listen to his own words: "I am the resurrection and the life: / whoever believes in me, / though he should die, will come to life; / and whoever is alive and believes in me / will never die." (Jn 11:25-26)

6 Psalm 35:9-10   Fullness of Life
I will rejoice in the Lord, / I will be joyful because of his salvation. / All my being shall say, / "O Lord, who is like you?"

We can never begin to comprehend the tremendous love which the Lord has for each one of us. Love wants to be closely united with the beloved. God loves us so very much that he wants us to be united with him for all eternity. He wants this more than we could want it ourselves, which staggers our imagination.

Jesus did everything possible to wipe out our sinfulness, to redeem us, and to open the way to heaven for us. What rejoicing fills our whole being when we hear Jesus summarize his whole redemptive love in these few words: "I came that they might have life / and have it to the full." (Jn 10:10)

7 Psalm 20:6   Glorious Victory
May we shout for joy at your victory / and raise the standards in the name of our God. / The Lord grant all your requests!

Jesus died to redeem us. He rose from the dead to share his divine life with us, so much does he love us. However, there is a limit to the life he can share with us as long as we are bound by our physical bodies.

In spite of this knowledge, a fear of death lurks within all of us. As we become more and more aware that death is the doorway into the fullness of his divine life and also into a union of perfect love with God and all our loved ones, then, with St. Paul, we can shout for joy at our victory: "Death is swallowed up in victory." "O death where is your victory? O death, where is your sting?" (1 Cor 15:54-55)

Joy to the World

Our Christian era began on a note of joy. In announcing the birth of John the Baptist, the angel said to Zechariah: "Joy and gladness will be yours, and many will rejoice at his birth" (Lk 1:14).

Soon after the angel announced the birth of Jesus to the shepherds: "I come to proclaim good news to you—tidings of great joy to be shared by the whole people" (Lk 2:10).

Knowing that God so loves us that he gave us his only Son to redeem us makes our heart overflow with great joy. This awareness gives purpose and peace, meaning and joy to everything we do.

The psalmist prepared the way for the fullness of our joy as he prayed and sang about the goodness and kindness, the love and compassion of our Father. Linger on his words and pray with the psalmist during these coming days.

1 Psalm 40:9 Joy in Giving
To do your will, O my God, is my delight, / and your law is within my heart!

There is great joy in giving. One of the most difficult gifts for us to give is our own will. Many of us are so entrenched in our own habits and convictions that any change is difficult.

It may require great generosity on our part to keep our will in conformity with the will of our loving Father. When we are able to do so, we will experience much peace and joy. Jesus shows us the way: ". . . it is not to do my own will / that I have come down from heaven, / but to do the will of him who sent me." (Jn 6:38)

2 **Psalm 119:111-112   Journey in Joy**
Your decrees are my inheritance forever; / the joy of my heart they are. / I intend in my heart to fulfill your statutes / always, to the letter.

Decrees and statutes were very important to the chosen people. Laws bound them together as the special people of God. Through his decrees and statutes, God was showing them the path to happiness in this life and a sure course to eternal union with him.

We, too, are special people. Jesus came as the way, the truth, and the life. We need nothing more than to follow him to reach our eternal destiny.

Certainly we will find much joy in Jesus' words: "If anyone would serve me / let him follow me; / where I am, / there will my servant be." (Jn 12:26)

3 **Psalm 63:8-9   Protective Wings**
That you are my help, / and in the shadow of your wings I shout for joy. / My soul clings fast to you; / your right hand upholds me.

These words attempt to describe the peace and joy of being protected by God. Words fail to describe our sense of intimate union with God and the sheer joy which such a closeness enkindles in us.

The psalmist uses a touching image of resting secure and protected in the shadow of God's wings. It speaks to us of resting content in the protective embrace of our Father's love. Jesus used the same image. May his lament never be spoken of us: "How often I yearned to gather your children, as a mother bird gathers her young under her wings, but you refused me." (Mt 23:37)

4 Psalm 92:5 Hands That Praise
For you make me glad, O Lord, by your deeds; / at the works of your hands I rejoice.

God is no farther away from us than our hands. Observe your hands! How wonderfully God has made them! They give us cause to rejoice "at the works of thy hands."

We can pick up a pin-size article or move a cumbersome object. Trained hands can paint a beautiful picture, type a flawless letter, or render a delightful concert on the piano.

Our hands express our prayer postures. We raise our hands to praise God. We plead our cause with uplifted palms.

St. Paul's pastoral advice is quite directive: "It is my wish, then, that in every place the men shall offer prayers with blameless hands held aloft, and be free from anger and dissension." (1 Tm 2:8)

5 Psalm 119:41 Humility Brings Joy
Let your kindness come to me, O Lord, / your salvation according to your promise.

Acknowledging our need for God's help is practicing real poverty of spirit. This frame of mind and attitude helps us to:
—recognize our own inadequacy
—acknowledge our human weakness
—admit our dependency on God.

This realization brings us a deeper, more joyful appreciation of the Father's protective and providential love which leads us to the joy which is eternal.

St. Peter reminds us of the proverb: "God is stern with the arrogant, but to the humble he shows kindness." (1 Pt 5:5)

6 Psalm 145:6-7 A Joyful Hosanna

They discourse of the power of your terrible deeds / and declare your greatness. / They publish the fame of your abundant goodness / and joyfully sing of your justice.

When our heart is brimful of joy and gladness, we are eager to break into song. Our countenance radiates the joy of our heart. Our lips smile readily; our eyes dance with glee; our voice breaks into a hymn of praise.

When we contemplate the Lord's abundant goodness to us, we want to sing joyfully. Our prayer and praise gladden the heart of our Father.

Jesus invites us to join his friends in their joyful homage: "Hosanna to the Son of David. . . . Hosanna in the highest!" (Mt 21:9)

7 Psalm 66:1-3 Shout Joyfully

Shout joyfully to God, all you on earth, / sing praise to the glory of his name; / proclaim his glorious praise. / Say to God, "How tremendous are your deeds!"

The tremendous deeds of God have created us, nurtured us, forgiven us, and continue to surround us at every moment of our existence. God's boundless love for each one of us impels him to continue his tremendous deeds as we journey down the pathway of life.

Knowing that we are loved so lavishly by our gracious Father, our hearts overflow with joy as they break out in glorious praise.

Sirach's advice is timely: "You who fear the Lord, hope for good things, / for lasting joy and mercy." (Sir 2:9)

WEEK FIFTY ONE

Joy without End

Joy is a God-given gift. Genuine, quiet, interior joy is one of the many fruits of the Holy Spirit. The source of our joy is the word of God and the message of love it conveys to us.

When we realize that God will never abandon or reject us but that he accepts us just as we are, our hearts are flooded with joy. This overflowing joy is only a foretaste of the joy awaiting us in heaven. The joy of Jesus is eternal.

Jesus revealed the Good News to us that we might experience genuine joy. He said: "All this I tell you / that my joy may be yours / and your joy may be complete." (Jn 15:11)

Let us ponder the joy awaiting us as we pray with the words of the psalmist.

1 Psalm 105:3-4 Look to Him
Glory in his holy name; / rejoice, O hearts that seek the Lord! / Look to the Lord in his strength; / seek to serve him constantly.

We "seek to serve him constantly" when we desire with all our heart the happiness of heaven. Such a fervent desire is a prayer in itself. When we persevere in this desire, it becomes stronger and stronger.

When St. Paul urges us to "pray without ceasing," he is encouraging us to desire without ceasing our union with God for all eternity.

St. Paul tells us we can depend on this: "If we have died with him / we shall also live with him; / If we hold out to the end / we shall also reign with him." (2 Tm 2:11)

2 Psalm 16:11   His Path
You will show me the path of life, / fullness of joys in your presence, / the delights at your right hand forever.

There is only one path of life which leads to genuine Christian joy, and that path is the one which Jesus mapped out for us in proclaiming the Good News.

Along life's expressway we find many signs, even billboard size, enticing us to compromise or even abandon Jesus' way of life. There are many easy exits along the highway of life, but they offer no return ramps. Following his way will not only fill us with joy in this life but will lead us to "the delights at his right hand forever."

St. Peter's words are a solemn promise: "Although you have never seen him, you love him, and without seeing you now believe in him, and rejoice with inexpressible joy touched with glory because you are achieving faith's goal, your salvation." (1 Pt 1:8)

3 Psalm 34:5-6   Be Radiant
I sought the Lord and he answered me / and delivered me from all my fears. / Look to him that you may be radiant with joy.

When we experience a deep awareness of the presence of the Lord, or when we recognize his gracious response to our needs, fear disappears from our hearts and we are filled with joy.

We beam with a radiance which only the peace and joy of the Lord can produce. Keeping our focus on the Lord will help us sustain this radiant joy. Jesus promised: ". . . you are sad for a time, / but I shall see you again; / then your hearts will rejoice / with a joy no one can take from you." (Jn 16:22)

4 Psalm 32:11   No Greater Joy
Be glad in the Lord and rejoice, you just; / exult, all you upright of heart.

Joy is not the absence of difficulties, disappointments, and dissension. Joy is rather the awareness of the presence of the Lord in our lives. Jesus loves us so much that he could not leave us but devised a way and a means of remaining with us in his glorified, risen life. This awareness makes our hearts sing for joy.

We are never alone. Jesus is with us always and everywhere. If we share our sorrow with him, it will be reduced by half. When we share our joy with him, our own joy will be doubled.

St. Paul's advice brings us joy: "The Lord is near. Dismiss all anxiety from your minds." (Phil 4:5f)

5 Psalm 35:27   Joyful Perseverance
Let those shout for joy and be glad / who favor my just cause; / And may they say, "The Lord be glorified; / he wills the prosperity of his servant!"

The greatest prosperity we could ever hope to achieve is to reach our final destiny—the eternal bliss of heaven. As we set and maintain our course along the path which Jesus mapped out for us, we will discover much peace and joy.

Along this course we will be sure to find a cross. Jesus assures us that if we take up our cross daily we will reach the joys which have no limit and no end.

Jesus himself tells us: "...the man who holds out till the end is the one who will come through safe." (Mk 13:13)

6 **Psalm 105:42-43   Promise of Joy**
For he remembered his holy word / to his servant Abraham. / And he led forth his people with joy; / with shouts of joy, his chosen ones.

These words of the psalm give us solid ground for the joy which should characterize the life of every Christian. Throughout salvation history, even from the time of Abraham, God has made some extravagant promises to us, his people. He has kept every single one of them. Can there be any greater source of joy?

Jude tells us how to prepare ourselves to receive the fullness of God's promise: "Persevere in God's love, and welcome the mercy of our Lord Jesus Christ which leads to life eternal." (Jude 21)

7 **Psalm 84:5   The Lord's House**
Happy they who dwell in your house! / Continually they praise you.

What an uplifting sight to pause and enjoy a celestial sunset. Its constantly changing hues and shades, its panoramic beauty, is beyond human description. Such an exquisite scene touches our soul. It rejoices our heart. It enkindles our spirit. It motivates us to break out in praise for the marvelous deeds of the Lord.

We need to remind ourselves that this is only a dim shadow of the divine majesty which we will behold when we enter into the presence of the Lord to glorify him for an eternity. St. Paul was right when quoting the prophet: "Eye has not seen, ear has not heard, / nor has it so much as dawned on man / what God has prepared for those who love him." (1 Cor 2:9)

Alleluia

Alleluia is a word which is formed by placing several abbreviated syllables together. It means PRAISE THE LORD. It is a brief prayer of praise which begins and ends many of our prayers.

Alleluia saturates the liturgy of the church especially during the Easter season. Its frequent recurrence is a constant reminder that our first duty is to praise and glorify the Lord.

The brevity of the word alleluia enables us to use it intermittently throughout the course of the day as an ejaculatory prayer. Praise is not only the first duty of every Christian but it is also the highest form of vocal prayer.

May our whole day be punctuated with ALLELUIA, PRAISE THE LORD!

1 Psalm 104:34 Theme Song
Pleasing to him be my theme; / I will be glad in the Lord.

When we recognize God's omnipotence and holiness as mentioned in this psalm, our hearts are light and joyous. We have a great desire to break into songs of praise. We can be certain that this theme is pleasing to him.

Singing our praise to God is a sublime form of prayer, since our focus is theocentric. It is a prayer of adoration. With the psalmist let us sing to the Lord all our life and continue to sing praise to our God while we live. "Through Jesus Christ may he carry out in you all that is pleasing to him. To Christ be glory forever! Amen. (Heb 13:21)

2 Psalm 106:48 Amen, Alleluia

Blessed be the Lord, the God of Israel, through all eternity! / Let all the people say, Amen! Alleluia.

The psalmist invites us to bless the Lord for all eternity. He prays that we and "all the people" will respond joyously with our "Amen."

Amen is a liturgical acclamation which not only expresses our agreement with what has just been said but which also carries with it a responsibility to implement what has just been verbalized. Our amen in this instant is our commitment to continue to bless the Lord, our God. St. Peter encourages us in this commitment: "Grow rather in grace, and in the knowledge of our Lord and Savior Jesus Christ. Glory be to him now and to the day of eternity!" (2 Pt 3:18). ". . . in all of you God is to be glorified through Jesus Christ; to him be glory and dominion throughout the ages. Amen." (1 Pt 4:11)

3 Psalm 144:9 Hosanna

O God, I will sing a new song to you; / with a ten-stringed lyre I will chant your praise.

Singing has always been an important part of the liturgy of the church. Singing is a powerful form of prayer. It has been said that singing has twice the value of recited prayer.

As the awareness of God's goodness wells up within us, we want to give it expression in song; to sing a new song "with a ten-stringed lyre." Our hearts may be so overjoyed that we sing a brand new song of praise with a new enthusiasm and intensity.

Let us join the friends of Jesus and sing with them: "Hosanna to the Son of David! / Blessed is he who comes in the name of the Lord! / Hosanna in the highest!" (Mt 21:9)

4 Psalm 146:10   Reign of Love
The Lord shall reign forever; / your God, O Zion, through all generations. Alleluia.

What a joy to know that God's reign will last forever. It is a reign of love. His love sustains us, energizes us, nourishes us.

The great mystery of his love is the truth that it is immutable, unchanging, regardless of what we do. He never withdraws his love, nor does he force his love upon us. He waits for us to be open and receive it. It is we who control his love. We can open wide to receive his love, or we can open slightly, or, God forbid, we can close ourselves to his love. "Blessed are you, and praiseworthy, / O Lord, the God of our fathers, / and glorious forever is your name." (Dan 3:26)

5 Psalm 147:1   Nothing More Fitting
Praise the Lord, for he is good; / sing praise to our God, for he is gracious; / it is fitting to praise him.

When we pause to reflect on the Lord's kindness and generosity to us and to all of creation, we are naturally moved to thank and praise our loving Father for he is goodness itself.

Praise and thanks evoke great joy within us. We are inclined to manifest that great joy outwardly as well. Proclaiming God's goodness gives him all the glory. "It is fitting to praise him."

The crippled man cured by St. Peter sets the pace for us. After being healed: "He went into the temple with them—walking, jumping about, and praising God." (Acts 3:8)

6 Psalm 147:7-8   Fields Shining

Sing to the Lord with thanksgiving; / sing praise with the harp to our God, / Who covers the heavens with clouds, / who provides rain for the earth; / Who makes grass sprout on the mountains / and herbs for the service of men.

As we strive to praise God, our hearts dance with joy. As we sing his praises we begin to multiply words in an attempt to describe the immensity of his goodness which provides the rain, the grass, and herbs for the service of men.

Our songs of praise burst forth with enthusiasm because God is worthy of all our praise for his countless benefactions to us.

Jesus reminds us that the spiritual harvest is ready to be reaped: "Open your eyes and see! / The fields are shining for harvest! / Others have done the labor, / and you have come into their gains." (Jn 4:35 and 38)

7 Psalm 147:20   Right Road

He has not done thus for any other nation; / his ordinances he has not made known to them. / Alleluia.

Ordinances are not merely laws and rules for us to follow but rather directives lovingly given by our Father to help us achieve genuine happiness. The Lord loves us. For this reason he has revealed ways and means for us to attain peace and joy in this life as a prelude to the eternal bliss awaiting us.

Our striving to follow these ordinances is pleasing to the Lord because he wants us united with him in heaven. Our striving to please him is a way of expressing our love for him. Jesus assures us: "You will live in my love / if you keep my commandments, / even as I have kept my Father's commandments, / and live in his love." (Jn 15:10)

Grand Finale

In this final hymn of praise, our whole being is completely absorbed in praising and glorifying our God for his mighty deeds and his sovereign majesty.

The psalmist calls for a full orchestra with every instrument contributing its own special sound of praise.

We, too, are invited to praise God with our whole being—mind, heart, soul, spirit, and voice—in one grand paean of praise to the majesty of God.

Psalm 150

Praise the Lord in his sanctuary,
  praise him in the firmament of his strength.

Praise him for his mighty deeds,
  praise him for his sovereign majesty.

Praise him with the blast of the trumpet,
  praise him with lyre and harp,

Praise him with timbrel and dance,
  praise him with strings and pipe.

Praise him with sounding cymbals,
  praise him with clanging cymbals.

Let everything that has breath
  praise the Lord! Alleluia.

Te Deum

You are God: we praise you;
you are the Lord; we acclaim you;
You are the eternal Father:
All creation worships you.
To you all angels, all the powers of heaven,
Cherubim and Seraphim, sing in endless praise:
Holy, holy, holy, Lord, God of power and
   might,
heaven and earth are full of your glory.
The glorious company of apostles praise you.
The noble fellowship of prophets praise you.
The white-robed army of martyrs praise you.
Throughout the world the holy Church
   acclaims you:
   Father of majesty unbounded,
   your true and only Son, worthy of all worship,
   and the Holy Spirit, advocate and guide.
You, Christ, are the king of glory,
the eternal Son of the Father.
When you became man to set us free
you did not spurn the Virgin's womb.
You overcame the sting of death,
and opened the kingdom of heaven to all
   believers.
You are seated at God's right hand in glory.
We believe that you will come, and be our judge.
Come then, Lord, and help your people,
bought with the price of your own blood,
and bring us with your saints
to glory everlasting.

Save your people, Lord, and bless your
    inheritance.
Govern and uphold them now and always.
Day by day we bless you.
We praise your name forever.
Keep us today, Lord, from all sin.
Have mercy on us, Lord, have mercy.
Lord, show us your love and mercy;
for we put our trust in you.
In you, Lord, is our hope:
and we shall never hope in vain.